in **DETAIL** Building in Existing Fabric

in **DETAIL**

Building in Existing Fabric
Refurbishment · Extensions · New Design

Christian Schittich (Ed.)

Edition Detail – Institut für internationale
Architektur-Dokumentation GmbH & Co. KG
München

Birkhäuser – Publishers for Architecture
Basel · Boston · Berlin

Editor: Christian Schittich
Co-Editor: Thomas Madlener, Andrea Wiegelmann
Editorial Services: Christine Fritzenwallner, Julia Liese

Translation German/English: Elizabeth Schwaiger (pp. 8–37), DETAIL (pp. 38–176)
Drawings: Norbert Graeser, Marion Griese, Olli Klein, Nicola Kollmann,
Emese Köszegi, Elli Krammer, Sabine Nowak, Andrea Saiko, Claudia Toepsch
DTP: Peter Gensmantel, Andrea Linke, Cornelia Kohn, Roswitha Siegler

This book is a cooperation between
DETAIL – Review of Architecture and
Birkhäuser – Publishers for Architecture

A CIP catalogue record for this book is available
from the Library of Congress, Washington D.C., USA

Bibliographic information published by Die Deutsche Bibliothek
The Deutsche Bibliothek lists this publication in the Deutsche Nationalbibliografie;
detailed bibliographic data is available on the Internet at <http://dnb.ddb.de>.

© 2003 Institut für internationale Architektur-Dokumentation GmbH & Co. KG,
P.O. Box 33 06 60, D-80066 München, Germany and Birkhäuser –
Publishers for Architecture, P.O. Box 133, CH-4010 Basel, Switzerland

Printed on acid-free paper produced from chlorine-free pulp (TCF ∞).

Printed in Germany
Reproduction: Karl Dörfel Reproduktions-GmbH, München
Printing and binding: Kösel GmbH & Co. KG, Kempten

ISBN 3-7643-1120-7

9 8 7 6 5 4 3 2 1

Contents

Creative Conversions

Christian Schittich

Working with existing buildings has long ceased to be only a question of preserving the city image and historic monuments; it has become an economic and ecological imperative. In a time, when resource and pollution issues are intensifying coupled with decreasing population numbers in the industrialized nations, working with the existing built environment, repairing and restoring it for continued use has become the order of the day, instead of destroying more green space and exploiting more resources. Conversions and upgrades – which, today, account for nearly 40 per cent of construction in Central Europe – will continue to gain in importance in the near future, accounting for a steadily increasing percentage of the total building volume.

Thus building in the built environment not only means working with historically valuable structures, but increasingly also with ordinary buildings – industrial structures or mass housing schemes from the postwar era. The spectrum of tasks is correspondingly varied: it ranges from simple repair to functional and aesthetic optimization or ecological upgrades, from restoration true to the original to creative conversion. In each case, the architect's approach is largely dependent on the old building itself.

For a long time, Carlo Scarpa's refurbishment of the medieval Castelvecchio in Verona (1956–1964) was considered the benchmark for all creative conversions. The principles, which Scarpa developed for the project – distinct separation of confident interventions and existing fabric through contrasting materials – have lost none of their validity to this day and continue to be applied far and wide in the treatment of historic monuments. Alvaro Siza's urban renewal in the Sicilian Saleme (see page 38ff) or the conversion of a church into a cultural center in Toledo by Ignacio Mendaro Corsini (see page 42ff) are examples that follow in the footsteps of Scarpa's tradition, albeit with fewer mannerist details.

What is more frequent, however, is a design philosophy where the boundary between old fabric and new completion is becoming increasingly blurred, where architects interpret the old building in a new way and develop it further. This is the case with the two spectacular conversion initiatives for monumental historic industrial sites – the former Bankside Power Station in London into the Tate Modern (see page 136ff) and the former Fiat factory in Turin (see page 144ff). Renzo Piano's approach to working with the impressive Lingotto factory can almost be described as pragmatic: seen from the outside, he has left the old building nearly untouched – with the exception of the two accents on the roof –, while much of the interior is characterized by an almost seamless merging between old and new, with the minimized details of the completion fitting naturally into the existing structure. Günther Domenig, on the other hand, has – metaphorically speaking – pierced the flesh of Nuremberg's massive old Reichsparteitag building (see page 156ff), achieving the feat of finding a practical use in the new documentation center for the cumbersome building, an important historic structure that should be preserved despite its negative historical legacy, without glossing over its past. While the form and appearance of the old structure have been largely preserved in the aforementioned examples, the renovation of housing schemes, especially the sterile panel construction in the former East, is focused not only on improving the quality of the living environment but also the aesthetic image, for example in the case of the balcony additions by Knerer and Lang in Dresden (see page 106ff). And finally, Baumschlager and Eberle have stripped the insurance building of the Münchener Rück down to the bare load-bearing structure, creating a modern building, which no longer reveals any traces of its predecessor on the inside or on the outside.

Architects have looked upon conversion and renovation as a necessary evil for a long time, preferring to make their reputations with spectacular new buildings. This was especially true during the classic modern era, when little value was attached to old buildings and the avant-garde focused all its energies on innovation. Things have changed, however. The examples mentioned above and the projects presented in this book reveal the broad spectrum of tasks, possibilities and attitudes in working with existing buildings and demonstrate that the theme is anything but dull. On the contrary: working with the given fabric, which imposes necessary constraints on the designer, is one of the most creative and fascinating tasks in architecture.

Conversions – the new normal

Johann Jessen and Jochem Schneider

The question of conversion is ubiquitous. The nuclear reactor in Kalkar, which never did 'breed', has been reconfigured into a congress and leisure center, a disused transformer station in Cologne now accommodates galleries, and the multiplex cinema in Freiburg's new main railway terminal is now being used for offices and a planetarium (Fig. 2.19). The list of transformations continues – and it is by no means limited to such extravagant solutions.[1] Conversion has reached everyday buildings and has not been restricted to heritage buildings for some time. Today one can operate on the assumption that anything and everything is available for conversion – there is no building that is a priori unfit for conversion. The future in planning and design lies above all in the area of the existing "mass product".

Urban development as modification of the built environment

Does the future task for architecture and urban design primarily consist in adapting and converting or even removing that which has already been built? Since the beginning of the 1970s, the percentage of investment in existing structures has been rising out of proportion in comparison with investment in new construction – with some economic variations. In the mid 1980s, more than half of all building funds were already devoted to existing buildings. Since then, the ratio continues to shift in favour of existing development.

Wherever prognoses predict further population decrease, fewer new apartments, kindergartens and schools will be required, but more seniors' residences and nursing homes. Drastic responses to the saturated market are being considered in the large cities in East Germany and also in other European regions, in some cases going so far as to propose the razing of entire housing developments. It also reasonable to assume that vacant industrial and housing schemes will, in future, be joined by vacant commercial and office buildings. Rationalization is going to have a forceful impact on this sector, especially the banking and insurance sector, and render office areas obsolete.
Finally, planning with existing buildings in mind – on a large and a small scale – is imperative also from an ecological perspective. Today, renovating and converting old buildings has become a key component in an urban planning strategy, which takes pride in responsible resource management. This has changed the way in which we look at existing buildings: the built city is viewed as a repository of massive amounts of material and energy. At the same time, the familiar patterns of urban development are still at work: in Germany, land use continues virtually unabated, with 120–130 hectares being consumed on a daily basis.[2]

Urban development has always meant urban expansion, conversion and maintenance all at once, albeit to differing degrees. Adapting existing structures to new requirements, as an alternative to demolition followed by new construction on developed land or undeveloped new building sites, is a constant in the changing urban environment. In pre-industrial times, the conversion of existing buildings for new uses was an economic necessity and a cultural norm. The technical effort and the time invested, the long usage cycle and value of a building demanded that one build for the long term and treat the substance with care. The limited availability of building materials, transportation methods that were often as laborious and expensive as demolition, made the "recycling" of building sites, sections and materials the rule.

From the perspective of how existing structures are treated in modern urban planning, one is tempted to interpret the era of urbanization beginning in the mid 19th century as an atypical, historic phase driven by a spirit of seemingly limitless, permanent expansion. The excessive value placed on the new was an expression of progress and prosperity. It went hand in hand with a profound rejection of history. In the context of urban planning, this attitude is documented in the speculative expansions, which accompanied the turbulent start-up and development of industrial expansion in the 19th century. In central locations, new department stores and office buildings replaced the old buildings and cast a new image across existing city cores. Whenever urban conversion was set as a public task, it was equivalent to speaking of demolition and new construction. Appreciation for old buildings was limited to classic monuments such as castles, churches and forts.

The low esteem for old buildings remained unchanged even after the First World War, on the contrary, new urban concepts – often designed in deliberate contrast to the old city – often led to the destruction of "superannuated" urban structures. This attitude persisted well into the 1960s of the 20th century and characterized European urban planning with a few exceptions. This is demonstrated not least of all by the fact that over 70 per cent of the existing development in Germany was created in the last five decades. Hence, renovation and conversion were seen by architects and planners as negligible exceptions, second-rate tasks.

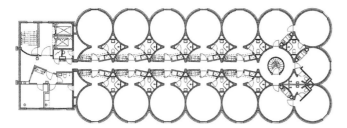

2.2

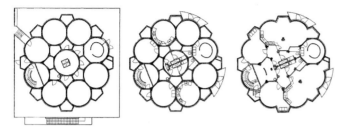

2.3

Urban planning with a greater focus on preserving and utilizing existing structures is a more recent phenomenon that is closely linked to the contentious shift in urban development from urban renewal to conservation at the beginning of the 1970s. Conservation, creating a city image and infrastructural improvements in renewal areas were the goals of these efforts; historic town cores and nineteenth-century residential districts near the city center were their targets. As urban renewal began to spread to villages, industrial and traffic wastelands, large housing complexes and – since the early 1990s – even former military installations, conversion was integrated into comprehensive urban planning strategies on the basis of economy and ecology. De-urbanization has since shed a stark light on another profound shift: conversion cycles have caught up with short lifecycles. People have come to recognize the advantages of temporary uses as part of a long-term strategy. The fact that this is not only a national issue is emphasized by the European research project "Urban Catalyst," which explores the interaction between planning goals and temporary cultural activities in urban renewal, for example, the planned intermediary use of the Palace of the Republic in Berlin (Fig. 2.9).

The structural adaptation of existing buildings has become one, perhaps even the central criterion for the future survival of our cities and urban regions. Conversion stands for economic use of materials, space and energy and is a contribution to better utilization of the infrastructure. In the meantime, it has also become a marketing tool for site promotion. Innovation and old building structure are no longer contradictions in term. There is no type of building or site that is not in principle suitable for renovation and conversion in the future. The architectural mass products of the past five decades are entering the stream of renewal with growing speed and increasingly shorter half-lives. In addition to the "facelifting" in large housing complexes, other examples of this trend are the upgrades to commercial and industrial areas with the arrival of service providers, the energy-related, structural and house- as well as media-related "retrofitting" of office buildings, the "relaunching" of pedestrian areas and shopping centers, to name but a few. Renovation and conversion are in demand as effective strategies for urban area and structure management. If they are to be directed at the apartment, office and commercial buildings erected in the second half of the 20th century over the long term, they must also become the focus of building and construction research. What does it take to achieve rational planning and building processes? How does one organize renovations in the built environment, given the lack of space for warehousing building materials and the urgent need for concepts for high-performance logistics? The conversion cycle encompasses not only mass-produced projects, but also cumbersome customized structures: functional buildings such as power plants, department stores, railway stations and laboratory buildings. In the meantime, people have converted former malting silos into homes, old settling basins into scuba diving pools, former churches into indoor basketball courts (Fig. 2.7) and gasometers into exhibition areas. Last but not least, the landscape itself is drawn into this process[3]: the landscape parks of the IBA-Emscher Park on the grounds of former steel works and of mining pits are eloquent examples. They were followed by similar projects at other heavy-industry sites and in brown coal mining areas. And in the shrinking cities of East Germany, some proposals go so far as to suggest returning former urban areas to nature.

Amortization periods are diminishing and conversion cycles have long since overtaken the defined periods for heritage protection. Today, buildings from the 1960s and 1970s are being adapted, modernized and refurbished for new uses. These are buildings, which generally do not fall into the category of heritage protection as we know it. Since they are usually treated with little respect, it is reasonable to assume that not a few testaments to that era have already been destroyed – a loss that will no doubt be felt one day. When new buildings are planned and erected today, there is an expectation that the sustainability, future flexibility and convertibility, in the sense of "prospective building management," of the development should be taken into consideration to ensure integration in material cycles that are as complete as possible.[4] Investors in specialized manufacturing and industrial projects, especially, are called upon to identify possible alternative uses in their building permit applications, in case the planned undertaking should turn out to be no longer economically viable as originally planned. These projects should be convertible, with reasonable effort, for a second or even third use, e.g. for office, apartment or other commercial uses. "When care is taken to select the appropriate structure and materials, it is possible to realize buildings that produce little construction waste, require low maintenance effort, are able to react flexibly to changes and can be nearly 100 per cent recycled at the end of their life cycle."[5] Investment calculations and permit processes should include not only the construction costs, but also

the entire demolition costs. This causes a shift in the parameters on which decisions are based: suddenly renovation and conversion look attractive even from an economic perspective. This will no doubt lead to a polarization with regard to new buildings: on the one hand objects with short amortization periods and limited life cycles and on the other, long-term investment objects, which incorporate adaptability for new uses that are still undefined at the moment of planning.

How are new uses matched with existing buildings?

Conversions result in a shift in the traditional relationship between object and use: whereas an envelope is usually designed for a given program in the case of new construction, this envelope already exists in structures for which new uses must be developed. The challenge and the potential of the task for planners, architects and clients lie in this reversal of the traditional definition. Since everyday, often insignificant buildings are also at their disposal in addition to heritage-protected, historically important buildings, one common question that arises is the choice of an appropriate program. For the integration of new uses into old buildings, we can determine three different patterns. In addition to

2.1   Headquarters of Münchner Rück, Munich; Baumschlager + Eberle, Vaduz
2.2   Student housing in former grain silo, Oslo (1953), 226 housing units on 16 floors, floor plan; HRTB AS Arkitekter MNAL, Oslo
2.3   Apartments in a former barley and malt silo, Copenhagen (1957), floor plan; Vilhelm Lauritzen, Copenhagen
2.4   Temporary skatebowl in a former airplane hangar, Eindhoven; Maurer United Architects, Eindhoven. Room for movement – the hangar is rehabilitated as an indoor skateboard park.

2.4

2.5

featured structures, whose special structural and spatial characteristics often suggest cultural uses, directly or indirectly, there are acquired and occupied buildings, which offer space for short-lived programs that cannot be realized elsewhere, as well as commercial structures, which have entered into the economic value added cycle of the real estate market.

Feature spaces – existing buildings as exhibition spaces
Conversion is still the most familiar route as the only method of preserving classic building monuments. The new, generally cultural, presents itself as an obvious solution: castles are turned into castle museums, casemates into military museums, tax sheds into city museums (see p. 58ff; visitor center in Criewen). Even conversions of manor houses into concert halls, churches into community centers or granaries into libraries, all represent heritage-protected buildings in the traditional sense where both the value of the structure and the new public function are indisputable. They are prestige projects that often play an important role for the cultural identity and historic consciousness of a town. This is a popular approach for conversion because it can be seen as proof of municipal politics in the interest of the people. These projects enhance the local cultural profile and can also take on economic importance if they become tourist attractions. In the meantime, however, more stringent limits have been imposed for the public use of historic buildings due to the high costs incurred by the state or municipal agencies.

Niches for pioneers – appropriated buildings
At the opposite end of the spectrum we find vacant buildings with little or no economic value, which are not deemed historically important – usually old industrial and manufacturing buildings. They offer opportunities that are not available elsewhere: large building volumes and low rents allow for new combinations of uses, individualistic spatial interpretations and unusual experiences of the available space. Visual artists were probably the first to discover old warehouses and manufacturing buildings as spacious and inexpensive studios; but cultural initiatives also pioneered the appropriations of depreciated buildings. Former factories were among the most popular choices for experiments with new habitation and communal living. Young entrepreneurs often seize the opportunity to utilize such buildings to make a rapid and inexpensive transition into self-employment. Appropriation and occupation can also occur in rather informal and temporary manners – for example, when skaters or ravers seize urban spaces for creative uses that deviate from intended purposes. Here, conversions are effected with little effort, all that is needed are a few tools such as ramps or boards (Fig. 2.4). Questions of design or architecture play a subordinate role, the premium is placed on the space itself, an aura of emptiness filled with one's own ideas. In recent years this phenomenon of squatting or occupation has extended from industrial areas to vacant service sector buildings.

Conversion as exploitation – marketing existing buildings
Niche phenomena rarely remain niches for long, as is well known, and informal appropriation are frequently forerunners or interludes. They open windows on new markets and reveal lucrative options of use. Conversion has become

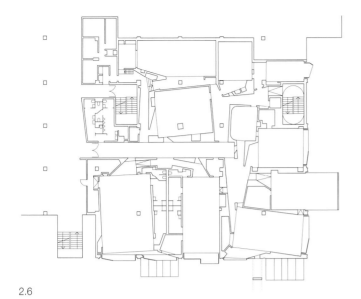

2.6

marketable, old buildings have been identified as vital capital beyond purely material estimated values.[6] Temporary users are forced to vacate and seek new niches somewhere else. The so-called "gentrification" of the then revalorized districts goes hand in hand with higher rents, changes to the mix of residents and businesses, and often a complete loss of the local identity. Conversion has in the meantime become an established sector of the real estate market, which is profiting from differentiated lifestyles and a growing appreciation for old buildings. Factory floors as company headquarters, barracks as hotels, silos as seniors' homes. Forms of habitation that began as outsider trends, such as living in lofts, have long since been assimilated as a new profitable segment and are presented to the general public in countless furniture catalogues. In large cities, the conversion of factories into condominiums for the upscale clientele has become one of the most lucrative real estate markets. Conversion has also become a marketable option and, a straightforward investment consideration from the perspective of the individual business, for retail or office uses with large area requirements, which had hitherto always been satisfied with new construction. In addition to material criteria, such as lower development costs, advantageous locations and generous space, immaterial criteria are also playing a key role in the decision-making process: "history" is becoming more important as a soft location factor. The prestige of anything deemed old or historic, the aura of authenticity in the tension field between new and old, serves as a stand in for innovation, imagination, openness and adaptability. Potential disadvantages, such as compromises in the spatial program or lower finishing standards, are accepted in turn. Even the clear risks, such as the difficulty to fully predict the effort in terms of cost and time or possible encumbrances as a result of preservation orders, no longer act as deterrents. There can be no greater proof of the reversal, which the perception of what innovation means has undergone from the "New New" to the "New Old" or rather the "Old New" than the fact that new building typologies are evolving from conversion. Today, developers are building new lofts because their multiplicity of uses is appreciated among tenants and owner-occupiers alike, especially in a time of lifestyles that are constantly in flux. The combination office with central communication and circulation zone, developed out of the necessity to work in buildings that did not have daylight in all areas, has mutated into a communicative and hence contemporary prototype of new construction. The experience that a large factory hall makes a wonderful museum suggests that the next new museum project should result in the construction of a large hall with an interior that allows for constant conversions, modifications and adaptations.

It is by no means a given, however, that there is an identifiable demand or rather functional concept for converted buildings. This is the case, for example, with specialized objects for which workable new uses are virtually impossible to determine and which would, at the same time, be too

2.5 Art college in the former library, St.Denis/Paris; facade by Bernard Dufournet and Jacques Moussafir
2.6 Floor plan of art college, upper floor
1970s buildings: fitting new structures into rigid construction grids. In the art college, old and new merge, spatial sequences arise in contrast to the old structure.

15

expensive to demolish – for example, bunkers – or other projects, which assume the function of creating an identity for the particular spatial context and which must therefore be preserved, for example gasometers or old manufacturing sites. In these cases, it is necessary to develop a function tailored to the building and the location in order to establish a new relationship between space and function. Conversions of grain silos into apartment buildings (Figures 2.2, 2.3), of a coking plant into an exhibition hall or a swimming pool into a library are examples of this type of project. The search for a concept that might be applicable to such difficult, massive buildings frequently culminates in hybrid uses, combinations that would be unthinkable in quite the same manner at any other location. The question of the right program, that is use, also arises in connection with the abundance of architectural inventory, which cannot make the claim of "exclusivity" because they are "mass products".

Conversion concepts of entirely ordinary buildings and ordinary subsequent uses, such as apartment or office buildings, are required at some locations. In Germany, this is a challenge that is currently prevalent in cities in the former East German states. In view of population forecasts, the question of what will happen to buildings erected in the past five decades is a fundamental one. At this time, there are no clear answers with regard to city planning and architecture. However, conversion should always be considered as a feasible alternative to demolition, recovery or modernization. The city of Paris has launched an unusual initiative, still untried in Germany, of converting office spaces that are no longer marketable – primarily buildings from the 1960s and 1970s – into low-cost subsidized housing. This initiative has been promoted through government sponsorship since 1994 and numerous projects have already been realized.[7] The growing share of more recent, convertible buildings is turning out to be unwieldy with regard to new usage concepts as a result of the specialized nature of this inventory in terms of minimization and prefabrication. In future, the consideration of which new program fits into an existing envelope, will not only become the focus of the debate among professionals, it will also assume social relevance as a public and civic task.

Aesthetic fundamentals of conversion

As the field of conversion is redefined and expanded, and given its intrinsic dissonance between old space and new use, established design principles are put in question. The traditional rule of "form follows function" is not the only one to be turned upside down when the new function is subjugated to the "giftedness of the space". It has become apparent that even the motto "contrast always works" has lost its formulaic meaning as a canonized adaptation of Carlo Scarpa's work, and has been replaced by an approach targeted to the particular object. The combination of old structures and new uses calls for specific solution depending on the relevant object and task. In other words, the genius loci is reinvigorated through conversion. Architects refer to history and interpret it individualistically.

The fact that a growing number of architects see conversion as a true design task and aesthetic challenge was not a foregone conclusion. That it is so, signals a shift in how the

2.7

2.8

profession sees itself and simultaneously explains the growing importance of this area for the practice. New construction is still considered the most rewarding discipline because it offers better, that is freer, opportunities for spatial design. Nevertheless, there is a growing number of protagonists who regard existing buildings as a profitable source of friction in the sense of a dialectical discourse – concurrent with the growing experiences of working with rehabilitation or renewal projects.

The design spectrum ranges from reconstruction of the old building true to the original condition, regardless of new uses, to carefree intertwining of Old and New and all the way to extensive dismantling followed by new additions. It ranges from the recreation of a destroyed image, to conservation of what still exists, to emphasis on the contrast between Old and New and all the way to complete redesign. In the case of conversion, design strategies break free from the "either-or" polarity of Old and New – they are always both. The status given to the old and the meaning assigned to the new – these are factors that depend on the concrete building task and the specific situation, but above all on the value, which the architect attaches to the relevant building beyond any preservation imperatives. What makes conversion attractive from a design perspective is precisely this integration of different historic layers. The new component does not establish an autonomous and independent meaning but always a dialogue with the existing elements. Since the architectural practice of conversion, much like the greatly expanded palette of uses, is extraordinarily varied today, it would be presumptuous and perhaps also incorrect to identify definitive aesthetic principles. Nor can one establish design approaches for specific building tasks, which prescribe a dependency between new function and design philosophy (form follows new function), or yet apply aesthetic concepts indiscriminately to existing buildings (form follows the existing). Hybrid forms and combinations are the norm. Even though the individual project in each concrete case is subject to the specific conditions resulting from the existing fabric, the brief, the intentions of the client and last, but not least, the architect's design, we can identify three different approaches and criteria for the creative treatment of existing buildings.

Preserving the Old in its entirety – seeking inspiration in the original
The desire to preserve and protect old buildings is the central point of departure for many conversions. Aesthetically, visual reference to the historic image of the original plays a decisive role. This approach, traditionally associated with heritage protection, seeks first and foremost to identify a new use that bears a close resemblance to the original intent or structure. A standard approach is to resort to cultural functions: castles are maintained virtually unchanged as museums showcasing the lifestyles of the aristocracy, old manor houses are used as libraries. The interior of the building is preserved and simultaneously opened to the

2.7   Sports and cultural center in former monastery church, Trier; Alois Peitz, diocese planning authority, Trier; Gottfried Böhm, Cologne; Dieter G. Baumewerd, Münster. The spatial configuration of the church is preserved, it is simply "reprogrammed" through interior modifications.
2.8   Lenbach House in Munich; Kiessler + Partner, Munich Urban infrastructure creates restful spaces – the design of the existing site is minimalist: entrance, display case and display window.

2.9

public. Preservation of the authentic structure is the goal of many local history museums or industrial museums, where the buildings themselves are the most important exhibits. The historic image of the building is seen as an important cultural icon in these cases, although the building does not remain unchanged. All structural interventions are subjected to the imperative of keeping changes to a minimum and practicing utmost restraint. In conversions undertaken in the spirit of conservation, the design ideal is to focus on authenticity and formal preservation of the "Old in its entirety". However, the idea of preserving the old substance in its entirety can also serve as a point of departure for -conceptual and design approaches that have more to do with restoration, which give precedence to an historic -ambience over the "pure" ambition for authenticity. They operate with traditional historic images, whereby the image of the apparently or truly historic is more interesting than the pursuit of authenticity. In these instances, the preserved envelope surrounds a completely different content, that is, interior and exterior are disengaged. The result is that the existing building is "perfected" and often appears more original than the original.

The opposite to this ideal of authenticity is the strategy of the controlled decay of buildings or monuments. Here the aesthetic focus is on an original, or rather on that which remains of the original. This strategy is employed when chances are low that an important monument can be preserved in the long term. Thus, the Völklinger Hütte, a former iron and steel works which was designated a world heritage site, has been exposed for some years to a process of continual erosion. The staging of disappearance and the finite nature of the object becomes an expression of "radical honesty".
The aesthetic concepts developed with explicit reference to the original are varied and contradictory. They range from strictly conservatory interventions into the existing fabric to the staging of an apparent historicity. However, all share the aesthetic idea of an image of the original, which determines the formal expression of the conversion as an "Old substance in its entirety".

Layers and fragments: the idea of difference
The second group of design strategies takes as the fundamental basis for their approaches the idea that Old and New discover their expression side by side in a converted building, where differing historic layers are brought into relation with each other. The idea of the homogeneous whole is replaced by a two- or multi-layered model, in which the space is composed of different fragments which only formulate a new whole as a result of their interaction. (p. 68ff, apartment and studio building in Sent). The new component is an obvious addition, clearly legible in the image and fundamentally different from the existing substance. A distance is created, a distance that is difference rather than dissonance. A spatial tension arises between the different temporal and iconic layers, which is identified and treated as a design theme. The individual stamp of the architect becomes manifest in how these differences are interpreted and how a new, and for the time being, final layer is added. Old and new are generally treated in an egalitarian manner, both undergo the same intensive treatment. The existing building is thus dissected into different historic layers in the course of the design process. The work of Carlo Scarpa is the stylistic model for this compositional strategy in working with existing buildings. No

2.10

building of the recent past offers a better illustration of the "art of the fugue" than the Castelvecchio in Verona (1956–1964).

The strategies aimed at emphasizing differences do not seek to completely revise the existing object. On the contrary, the historic structure is seen as an opportunity for reinterpretation. This attitude operates on the principle of the collage, contrasting different, distinct set pieces, which usually appear in a common context. The choice of materials underscores this differentiation: steel, glass and concrete symbolize the new in contrast to masonry, natural stone or simple plaster. Crafted details take on prime importance in this differentiated treatment of individual elements.

The conversion of "awkward" monuments poses an especially delicate challenge. An exemplary solution is found in the "strategy of difference" employed for the documentation center on the former Nazi parade grounds in Nuremberg[8] (p. 156ff). Regardless of whether the outcome are minor interventions or comprehensive principles applied to a far-reaching redesign, and independent of scale, this attitude is found in almost all ambitious architectural conversions of the 1980s and 1990s.

The existing fabric as material for the "new entity"
Constant reevaluation of existing fabrics also reveals ever-new perspectives of uses for seemingly depreciated or trivial buildings. In recent years, this context has translated into a growing trend to preserve ordinary buildings, which would previously have been slated for demolition without questions being asked: simple functional buildings without representational character or symbolic value. The decisions to preserve the existing structures for new projects are increasingly driven by straightforward, pragmatic reasons, for example economic considerations or zoning restrictions.

The area of working with mass-produced architecture, which does not fit into any category of heritage protection or cultural architectural importance, has given rise to a third fundamental design attitude: to regard the existing building as freely available and changeable "building material" and to use it directly in order to fashion a "new entity". The transition between existing structure and addition is seamless, the threshold between old and new building fluid – there is no joint. The existing fabric can be manipulated and interpreted at will, there are no constricting guidelines or laws and no "demand for authenticity". While the original identity remains recognizable, the resulting object is completely transformed. There is no exaggerated emphasis of the old in order to contrast it with the new, rather an instance of the "merging" that has entered into the debate on architecture. This type of assembly is neither distinctively old nor distinctively new; instead it encompasses both without rendering either legible as category or layer. The converted building presents itself

2.11

2.9 Former People's Chamber (GDR), Palace of the Republic, Berlin
The ruin is brought to new life as an experimental space, "Urban Catalyst" study, Berlin.
2.10 Ufa-palace in Freiburg; Harter + Kanzler, Waldkirch/Haslach; inaugurated in 1998, closed in 2001, converted in 2002 – rapidly changing markets lead to ever shorter usage cycles. The former cinema now houses offices and a planetarium.
2.11 Gallery in an old transformer station, Cologne; b&k + kniess, Cologne Transformation – the existing structure is adapted to the new use.

2.12

as a homogeneous whole. The result of this design approach is often original precisely because it is not original. It is more and more common to employ design concepts, which operate on the basis of removing as much of the existing building envelope as possible: buildings are dismantled right down to the load-bearing structure, completed where necessary and then simply clad in a new internal and external skin. These conversions are rarely identifiable as such and take on the appearance of new constructions. In view of the growing number of ordinary buildings, which are potential candidates for such measures, a range of design strategies is being developed. A poll of architects reveals that the differentiation strategy has lost its dominant position and has become simply one option among others. The concept of the "new entity" hints at an aesthetic approach, which responds not only to the qualities and unique properties of the substance but also to the specific nature of the project. The old is no longer treated as a stage to showcase the new. The goal is to seek a concept of design coherence beyond the categories of old and new.

The role of the architect – project developer and designer

What does conversion mean for the architect's work? The conversion of an ordinary old building presents the architect with a completely different challenge than new construction projects. For in this case design is above all finding a creative approach to working with the existing material. The comprehensive image evolves from the exploration of what already exists, and it is simply not impossible to create a new object cast "from a single mold". In this sense, the converted building is always characterized by a complexity and ambiguity in terms of material, time and content; many elements are already in place and must simply be absorbed or integrated. What is required is less an ability to invent, than one to reassign and interpret. This leads to a new understanding of the object: conversions are hybrids that are contradictions in themselves. They are in opposition to the view that designing is an individual creative act, to the idea of a newly designed, homogeneous and autonomous object. A work is developed in the field of tension between old and new, which is not identifiable as an individual achievement in the traditional sense: it is irrevocably inscribed with the signatures of shared authorship. Despite obvious interactions, program and design are also treated as consecutive processes in conversions. Whether the desired program can be implemented or requires some verification is often only revealed when the process is already underway. The definition of uses is directly and necessarily intertwined with questions of design. Design work on existing structures therefore requires a "dispositional ability" when clearly defined situations must be interpreted in direct contrast to their original or actual reading in order to create the basis for their continued existence. It is a matter of discovering a multitude of qualities in the "already finished product," beyond a superficially inscribed unambiguity of the object, and to express them in a new form with the means of design. This "art of observing" reveals ambiguous and varied readings of the apparently fixed old substance, which makes the creative consideration for a new designation possible in the first place. This conversion to another purpose blurs the contours of a building's "hour of birth". It is constantly reinvented and tells not only one but many stories. This overlap of project development

20

and design marks a central field of responsibility in which architects can play an important role in the future. Given their experience and knowledge of design, they are able to develop new and appropriate use options for existing spaces. At the same time, they have the required competence to assess the suitability of existing buildings. This combination of economic parameters, existing spatial qualities and design options opens up a new field of work, which cannot be left solely in the hands of location scouts, developers and project managers. Architects are needed, even before the actual design work begins. Design work for existing buildings addresses the issue of combinations of use. To hedge investments for the long term, architects must interfere proactively in "phase 0".

Notes:
This contribution is based on a study carried out by the authors on request for the Wüstenrot Foundation; cf: Wüstenrot Stiftung (ed.): Umnutzungen im Bestand. Neue Zwecke für alte Gebäude. Stuttgart/Zurich 2000. The authors would like to thank the Stuttgart architects Fritz Auer, Giorgio Bottega and Henning Ehrhardt, Peter Cheret, Boris Podrecca and Wolfgang Schwinge for their willingness to participate in extensive dialogue with regard to their experiences with conversions. Many tips and suggestions from those conversations have found their way into this contribution.

1   Current overview of conversions in: Powell 1999, Wüstenrot Stiftung 2000, Jester/Schneider 2002
2   Dosch 2002: p. 31ff
3   Baumgartner/Biedenkapp 2001
4   Kohler 1999, Sieverts 2000
5   Andrä/Schneider 1994: p. 151
6   Schlote, et al., 2000
7   Fachatte/Jaquand 1997, Lombardini 1997
8   Ghiringhelli, et al., 2001

2.13

Bibliography
1   Andrä, H.-P.; Schneider, R.: Recycling am Bau. Ressourcenminimierung bei Abbruch und Umnutzung. In: Deutsche Bauzeitung 11/1994, pp.144–151
2   Baumgartner, C.; Biedenkapp, A. (eds.): Landschaften aus Menschenhand. Die touristische Nutzung von (Industrie-)Kulturräumen. Munich 2001
3   Dosch F.; Auf dem Weg zu einer nachhaltigen Flächennutzung. In: Information zur Raumentwicklung 1/2002, pp. 31–45
4   Fachatte, R.; Jaquand, C.: Die Umwandlungen in Paris – eine Analyse. In: Bauwelt 31/32/1997, pp.1724–1729
5   Ghiringhelli, C.; Meier, H.-R.; Wohlleben, M.: Geschichte aufheben. Über das verändern von Bauten unter dem Aspekt der Sinn-Gewinnung. In: Die alte Stadt 2/2001, pp.77–91
6   Hassler, U.; Kohler, N.; Wang, W. (eds.): Umbau. Über die Zukunft des Baubestands. Tübingen/Berlin 1999
7   Kohler, N.: Modelle und Lebenszyklus des Gebäudebestands. In: ibid., pp.24–38
8   Jester, K./Schneider, E.: Weiterbauen. Erhaltung – Umnutzung – Erweiterung – Neubau. Berlin 2002
9   Lombardini, M.: Wohnen im Bürohaus. Programm und Finanzierung von Bauvorhaben der RVIP. In: Bauwelt 31/32/1997, pp.1720–1721
10   Powell, K.: Architecture Reborn. The Conversion and Reconstruction of Old Buildings. London 1999
11   Schlote, A.; Lederer, M.-M.; Lemke, H.-J. (eds.): Immobilien-Praxis. Spezial. Altimmobilien: Revitalisierung, Umnutzung oder Neubau? Mit Praxisbeispielen. Berlin 2000
12   Wüstenrot Stiftung (ed.): Umnutzungen im Bestand. Neue Zwecke für alte Gebäude. Stuttgart/Zurich 2000
13   Sieverts, T.: Konzepte und Strategien städtebaulicher Revitalisierung und Umnutzung des Gebäudebestands und der brachgefallenen Flächen als Teil einer systematischen Kreislaufwirtschaft. In: ibid., pp. 98–118

2.12   Palais de Tokyo, Paris; art, exhibition and event space in a former fair hall from 1937
Reassigning instead of renovating: in the Palais de Tokyo, interior spaces are treated as public exterior spaces.
2.13   Living and working in the washing plant at Wollishofen; Angélil/Graham/Pfenninger/Scholl Architecture. Existing building as material – in this plant, the original buildings are no longer recognizable after the conversion.

There's nothing green about building in the countryside

Günther Moewes

Building in the open country is the opposite of building in a built environment. And there is nothing ecological about it. New development areas increase land use and traffic and seal off more ground. Increased land use not only translates into a negative impact on the fauna that remains, it also, and especially, means that the last areas where people can experience nature and spend leisure time in a natural environment and the remaining regeneration areas are destroyed. Building in the open country consumes considerably more energy than building within an existing built environment.

Building in the open country was the urban planning strategy of society in times of economic expansion. Rapid urban growth was a product of population growth, of the shift from the rural agrarian society to the urban industrial society and of increasing space requirements per capita. Today, these reasons no longer apply to the industrialized countries of Europe: population figures are barely maintained as a result of higher life expectancy and immigration. Populations no longer decrease as a result of migration imposed by farm failures. And the living space requirements per capita are approaching their limit in terms of the effort required for heating, cleaning and maintenance alone. Most importantly, however: disused land, building gaps, industrial wasteland and conversion areas within the developed areas have surpassed the area required for new development for decades to come.

Building in the open country continues only because the economic and political forces in industrialized countries strive to artificially maintain the growth of the last century, despite saturated demands and population decrease: if a city with 100,000 housing units adds 4000 new units each year, bureaucratic economists read the outcome not as four per cent growth but as zero growth. In their eyes, this is a crisis. Only exponential increase is true growth. Thus, in start-up periods economic growth invariably plots a harmless horizontal line and shoots up along a steep vertical curve in the later stages of development.

Today, we are in such a late stage of economic development. Unfortunately the only curve that is rising sharply is that of private assets in Germany at an annual rate of 7.45 per cent having surpassed the four billion Euro mark. And with it, the other side of this list of balances per account, the curve of public debts. The concrete economic growth, on the other hand, lags behind as a result of saturated demand. This ever-growing divide dominates the economy and the building industry of today. Private surplus is ceaselessly poured into the landscape. Since 1960, land development has grown at a rate that is four times higher than population growth. In Germany alone, 130 hectares of land are consumed by new construction per day. And the utilization of urban areas has diminished at the same rate. Vast areas remain undeveloped in the centres of many large cities since the Second World War because hoarding property yields higher profits than developing these sites in a market characterized by constant price increase. The proportion of inner city wasteland or sparsely planted areas is growing constantly.

Existing fabric or vacant building?
As private surplus increases exponentially so does the pressure to invest, and as growth diminishes, unemployment increases. It is increasingly difficult to compensate for both of these factors through real demand and real production. They must be constantly fed artificially through disposable products, planned wear and tear, planned repair on all levels – and in construction this means demolition. In Germany, we were confronted with the concept of the throwaway society for the first time in the 1950s. In disbelief and highly sceptical we heard that people no longer darned socks in the United States, they simply tossed them out because it was cheaper to do so. Later on, we would hear the sock argument during every demolition debate: building a new house is cheaper than renovating. Little did we know that our scepticism would one day be called ecological.

The rejection of the built environment is also enshrined in the ideology of functionalism, which held that true modernity was only possible out in the open, far away from the Old. This was generally interpreted as a laudable spirit of departure and pioneering. In truth, it was simply a product of the victory of a one-track economic philosophy over the inclusive national economy that had reigned up until that point: division of labour, rationalization, separation of functions, meaningless functioning in a heteronomous work setting, cutting staff purely on the basis of economic calculations, detached solitary boxes, point-by-point competition and disassociated self-presentation. There was no room for consideration and careful integration into the existing fabric. Examples such as the J. J. P. Ouds Café De Unie in Rotterdam (1924) and Johannes Duikers Cineac in Amsterdam (1934) were the exception.

Realistically, we should have been living within the existing framework for some time. No one can convincingly explain why a population that is steadily decreasing despite immigra-

3.2

tion continues to need new buildings and to consume the last remaining landscapes or why this population cannot function sensibly in the existing built environment. Increasingly, new buildings are not built to satisfy a real demand but to counter-act unemployment.

Since 1990, 600,000 apartments have been built in East Germany alone, although there were 400,000 vacancies at the time. Today, the number of vacancies has soared to 1.3 million. That represents 15.8 per cent of the existing structures. Nevertheless, by the year 2001 new housing construction was still subsidised to the tune of 3.1 billion DM (1,6 billion Euro), whereas rehabilitation and renovation of old buildings received only 1.7 billion DM (870 million Euro) in public funds. Home equity contributions are still higher in Germany for new homes than for older homes.[1] There are only a few large cities in West Germany with a true housing shortage of roughly 100,000 units per year including replacement demand, while Kassel and Hanover, for example, record 13 and 8.2 per cent vacancy, respectively. In East Germany, entire housing developments are being stripped or demolished. At the same time 1.7 million m2 of office space stood vacant in Germany in 2002.

According to the retail association there is also a surplus of roughly 40 million m² retail space and roughly 15 000 retail operations were forced into closure in 2002 alone according to the association. With 105 million m², Germany already has 1.6 times more retail space per capita than Great Britain, for example.

3.3

Shopping centres located far from the downtown cores are the worst outcome of this development. Naturally, they cannot compel people to buy more. At best, the purchasing power remains the same. It is simply withdrawn from the built environment and pulled out into the open country. Big business thus destroys small and medium-sized firms and drives formerly self-employed entrepreneurs into an existence as low-wage sales associates in artificially lit and air-conditioned discount architectures.

The result is not only destroyed lives, but also destroyed buildings. The architecture of vacant old buildings is generally better and far more solid than that of new commercial buildings in and outside of cities, still, they are gradually falling into disrepair. Until the day comes when the mayor or the local press single them out as a sore in the town's image and no one can protest their demolition. The investors, however, move on to other pastures after 15 years, leaving an expensive conversion area behind, which then has to be renovated with tax money. And none of this is the result of inevitable economic facts but rather of self-inflicted and avoidable political mismanagement: dependence on commercial taxes forces communities to sell attractive and cheap land for development to potential tax payers, thereby diminishing the occupancy and value of their own cores. Development in rural areas, in villages, is an especially dark chapter. Instead of converting abandoned farms generously into living space (Fig. 3.3), they are burdened with conversion restrictions that hinder any sensible use. Villages are falling into ruin, only useful as backdrops for documentary films or films about the former GDR. At the same time, new single-family homes for the fugitives from urban life pop up row upon row. Fields are simply re-zoned as building land – there's always profit to be made in these schemes. The same pattern reigns wherever one looks: private capital invested into cheap land while valuable existing buildings decay.

Development in the country is the opposite of energy conservation

Renovation and ecological urban conversion, on the other hand, could create employment and keep the construction industry going for at least a decade. Conversions for energy conservation alone require € 340 billion in Germany according to the calculations of national economic institutes. Spread out across ten years that would result in € 34 billion per year. In 2001, new housing projects were still funded to the tune of € 1.59 billion, renovation projects received € 0.85 billion in subsidies. As we have seen, much of this only served to increase the number of vacancies. This is exacerbated by the home equity subsidies for new versus old homes. If these incentives were directed at promoting efficiency measures in old buildings, the missing 31 billion of private means could easily be mobilized on an annual basis. With these € 340 billion it would be possible to gradually evolve towards building energy savings of up to 75 per cent, representing roughly 24 per cent of total primary energy consumption.

In other words, energy conservation means: converting existing buildings. Indeed, there are only three building measures that truly conserve energy, that is, measures where energy consumption is lower after construction than before: renovation, replacing old buildings with more energy-efficient new buildings and closing building gaps. All of these are measures on existing structures.

As a rule of thumb, every building gap wastes roughly the same amount of energy as the number of floors on either side. By comparison to a standard apartment surrounded by other units on all sides, an apartment facing a building gap has an additional loss area, through which as much energy is wasted as on the front and rear facades of the apartment, that is roughly 50 per cent of the total requirement of a fully enclosed unit. Given a building gap across four floors, this means a 50 per cent loss from altogether eight apartments on either side of the gap – or a total loss of 100 per cent for four apartments.

The number and impact of buildings gaps are underestimated. In old residential districts from the foundation period with block edge development, it is not unusual to encounter 70 building gaps per km², that is, given an average four-story building height, a waste of the heating requirements of 280 uninsulated apartments for uninsulated gables, and of 280 insulated apartments for insulated gables. But that is not all. For the energy requirements of the apartments of the new building, which is erected to close the gap, are considerably lower than the requirements in detached new buildings. Building gaps are not only undeveloped lots. Nor do they have to reach all the way down to the ground. A single-story supermarket between two five-story buildings wastes not only heating

3.4

Captions
3.1 Apartment and commerce building in a 2.56 m wide building gap, Cologne, 1997; Arno Brandlhuber + Bernd Kniess, Cologne
3.2 Single family home neighbourhood near Dresden
3.3 Conversion of a former stable into a duplex, 1997, Bergün, Switzerland; Daniele Marques and Bruno Zurkirchen, Lucerne
3.4 Parasite on top of the Las Palmas warehouse, Rotterdam 2001; Korteknie & Stuhlmacher, Rotterdam (p. 98ff)

energy, but also space for the four floors above the supermarket, which we then encounter somewhere in the countryside outside of the city.

At times, building gaps are deliberately maintained in order to connect green space, provide access to courtyards resulting from reductions to the urban density or because windows that were set illegally into the adjacent gables after the war have established new rules by default. What such misguided decisions fail to take into account is that green spaces can be linked and access can be provided to courtyards without difficulty when the gap is closed, by the simple expedient of creating an arched gateway at ground level as was common practice in the 1920s.

Aside from insulation, the closing of building gaps represents the second highest savings potential in building upgrades and renovation. It not only saves energy, it generally also preserves landscape. And it is not only limited to historic block edge developments. Modern post-war architecture is an area that is often overlooked in this context. It too, is existing architecture that has reached the stage where renovation and upgrades are necessary. There are few other applications where upgrades that address social, aesthetic and energy-conservation issues can be combined with similar success. For modern architecture attained the height of generating energy wasting surfaces. These buildings are often veritable monuments to energy wasting surfaces. When the energy problem reached a hitherto unknown scale as a result of increased fossil fuel consumption, energy waste also soared in architecture like never before. The new urban principle was 'detached'

3.5

building: point, line, hill and endless rows of detached single-family homes. Whereas block edge development had only had two external walls, the new buildings had four.

But the key word was 'functional separation': no more multi-functional agglomerations of buildings, but a separate, free-standing building for each purpose. All the retail stores, supermarkets, kindergartens, car showrooms and small businesses, which could have been easily accommodated on the ground floors of multi-story buildings, were spread across the landscape as 'freestanding' single-story structures. What had been energy neutral ceilings became vast, useless and energy-wasting flat roof areas. If one were to regard these areas as potential building lots and actually develop them, one would preserve not only landscape but also conserve energy. Building apartments on top of the flat roofs in commercial districts would also result in a plethora of other synergetic effects: spacious roof terraces instead of small balconies stuck onto the facade, dual use of parking lots, reduced development effort and so forth. Nevertheless, this theme is thus far limited to student projects. There are few real examples, and the conversion potential is vastly underestimated (Figures 3.1, 3.6).

The picture is more encouraging with regard to the renovation of housing schemes and multi-story buildings. As far back as 1986, I developed a model for the energy-conscious renovation of the large housing scheme of Dortmund-Scharnhorst with my students. This was as residential development with four-story panel constructions, an urban planning crime of the 1960s, as the press put it. The students simply closed all gaps into complete block edge developments. In doing so, they

noticed that most of these housing schemes are in essence no more than disguised block edge developments, into which artificial gaps had been planned as recently as the 1990s to satisfy a need for modern openness. Since then, there have been numerous successfully realised rehabilitations of such neighbourhoods or even of administration buildings. The catalogue of interventions invariably matches the one developed in the student project in 1986: closing gaps or open corners, adding a new, light and recessed floor, fronting facades with a scaffold of balconies, winter gardens or glass fronts (Figures 3.5, p. 110ff).

Closing building gaps and roof additions are renovation measures that involve new construction. In addition, there are others that are straightforward energy conservation measures. Listed in the sequence of their energy-saving potential, these are:
• Insulation (exterior walls, windows, roof)
• Warm water production with collectors
• Courtyard glass enclosures (atria)
• Passive use of solar energy
• Power production by means of photovoltaics
Insulating old buildings remains a problematic task: since the insulating layer should always be an external feature, it destroys the character and aesthetics of historic facades, especially those of foundation period buildings, classic workers' housing and brick facades. This problem also can't be solved by developing new materials. Another problem, often underestimated and ignored in standard instruction manuals is that insulation offers an ideal habitat for all kinds of rodents: rats and mice penetrate all the way to the upper floors, attics and roofs of multi-story buildings, where they are no longer controlled by the presence of natural predators. This in turn leads to the spread of tons of toxins, which cannot break down. It is often impossible to completely seal old buildings.
Glass enclosures above courtyards can reduce the transmission losses through the building skin and save roughly 20 per cent in heating costs – an option that is generally underestimated. One can also envision glass enclosures, which can be opened in summer. Another overlooked alternative is temporary insulation: highly-insulated folding or sliding shutters can be closed at night – that is, 50 per cent of the time in winter.

Developing the built environment should not be understood as a mere aesthetic integration task. It is more important than ever to see it as an element of an overarching strategy of ecological urban conversion. Ecological urban conversion of this kind should not only save heating energy in a 'defensive' manner, it should be employed pro-actively to generate solar energy, above all solar power and warm water. Why should solar power continue to be generated predominantly in rural settings on elaborate structures erected specifically for that purpose, while building surfaces in cities remain unused? All roofs and south facades should be regarded as solar surfaces that are available free of cost. Not as carrier surfaces on which modules are installed after the fact, but as structurally integrated solar skins, conceived as such from the outset, and as passive solar glazing. Conversion and renovation would suddenly assume a new high-tech character. Inserted new buildings would no longer be discernible from old buildings. Desolate concrete jungles would be transformed into modern high-tech districts. This would be the true solar city of the future, and it would not rise in the open countryside but from the existing built environment.

3.6

Note:
[1]   At time of printing, new rules on home ownership and ecological subsidies were being discussed in the German parliament, including the potential for greater subsidies for existing buildings.

Captions
3.5   Rehabilitation of a housing complex in panel construction, Leinefelde/Thuringia, 2000, closure of an open corner; Meyer-Scupin and Petzet, Munich
3.6   Conversion of a soap factory, Zurich, 1997, mixed use with trades, studios and apartments; Kaufmann, van der Meer and Partner, Zurich

Preservation of Buildings from the Modern Era

Berthold Burkhardt

In recent years a number of important buildings dating from the classic Modern have been restored, for example the buildings designed by the two Bauhaus directors Walter Gropius and Hannes Meyer in Dessau, the Einstein tower by Erich Mendesohn in Potsdam, the Lange House by Mies van der Rohe in Krefeld and the Schminke House by Hans Scharoun in Löbau/Saxony, as well as several housing schemes by the brothers Taut in Berlin and Magdeburg. To this, we can add a list of important buildings in neighbouring European countries, such as Sonneveld House by Brinkman and van der Vlugt in Rotterdam. These projects have reinvigorated the dialogue on the intentions and the influence of modern architecture and urban design, and on the methods employed to renovate them. Diverging conservatory attitudes and different renovation techniques define today's practice of preserving buildings from the modern era. Questionable solutions of renovating a building in its original image, often unknown in its entirety, come face to face with preserving a building and telling its story through visible traces. To renovate and upgrade buildings from the modern era with the latest methods of technology is not only a denial of the importance of the history of building technology, it is also often a question of what is suitable for the building as a whole.

The architects of the modern era were open to aesthetic and structural experimentation, but it would be wrong to group all their buildings into the category of experimental architecture. The modern housing schemes of Otto Haesler in Celle and Bruno Taut in Magdeburg and Berlin, and not least of all Hans Scharoun's Schminke House in Löbau, were surely not intended as "projects with expiry dates". After all, extant buildings from that era have reached a life span of over seventy years, not because they have been protected by heritage orders but because of their proven utility and sustainability.

In renovating, preserving and in some cases converting buildings from the classic modern, heritage protection has stepped into a new area in terms of technology. Industrialized products, machine and manual production and installation processes, as well as the resulting hitherto little known conditions and requirements in terms of building physics and climate present new challenges in the practice of heritage conservation.

The knowledge of historic concepts for climate control and the chemical reactions of building materials, but also of user behavior in earlier times is a valuable basis for the preservation of building monuments. It is also essential for buildings, which are not protected by heritage conservation orders and which require renovation or upgrades imposed by new uses or existing damage. By exploring historic, technical and functional themes and the changing interactions between them, the insights gained from this can be applied in exemplary fashion to individual buildings and heritage conservation can make an important contribution to the preservation of the built environment as a whole.

The modern movement in architecture in the Germany of the Weimar Republic coincided with the staggering progress in technology and industrialization. The evolution in construction and building technology at the time – industrially manufactured building materials and components, new energy sources such as electricity and gas, and new supply and disposal systems for heating and water – changed the city and the house within a few decades to a far greater degree than new architectural attitudes or styles. The architects of the modern era were especially interested in new products and processes, which they assumed would support their reform ideas. The practice revealed the problems that are inevitably linked to such a turbulent period of development, no doubt also noticeable in shortcomings and the wear and tear in individual examples. One of the architects of the Weißenhofsiedlung in Stuttgart, the then chief city architect of Rotterdam J. J. P. Oud, commented critically: "It is wrong to generalize that technology is greatly advanced, this may be the case in the manufacture of small goods, but in building, technology is too backward to execute what we want to do." [1]

However, the new building systems did enable the technical realization of the cubist-geometrical architectural vocabulary of Gropius or Mies van der Rohe, or the freer, organic forms of Scharoun or Mendelsohn. Be it reinforced concrete floors or iron girders – for the first time in the history of architecture, it was possible to construct buildings of free-standing panels with flat ceilings across wide spans and cantilevered roofs. Mies van der Rohe designed the internationally admired German pavilion for the World's Exhibition in Barcelona in 1929 with flat ceiling slabs and wall panels, and in 1937 Hans Scharoun wrote about his house in the Weißenhofsiedlung: "House 33 was created out of pleasure in playing with the new materials and the new spatial challenges." [2]

The use of new or improved building materials such as concrete, iron, glass, plastics or material combinations not only made new building forms possible, it sometimes also imposed changes, and in part even a completely new approach to planning and executing construction projects. Trades concerned with building systems (heating, sanitation and electrical installations) emerged as entirely new sectors, while traditional trades experienced a loss of skilled workers. Thus carpenters worked as form-workers in reinforced steel and iron construction. The structural change and the increased activity in communal, collective as well as commercial and industrial construction gave rise to large construction firms that worked nationally or even internationally in contrast to the traditional local trades.

Gropius countered with the demand that skilled trades must be the indispensable foundation for industrialization and prefabrication. He sought to promote a reform, where trade and industry would unify and continue to develop in partnership: "It is an intrinsic character of the human spirit to constantly improve and refine his tools, to mechanize material work processes and to gradually facilitate intellectual work. Today's trade and industry are engaged in a continuous process of growing closer and must merge fully with one another into a single entity of work, which once again gives every individual the sense for collaboration on the whole and hence the spontaneous will to participate in it. In this united entity of work, the skilled trade of the future will be the experimental field for industrial production, speculative experimental work would create standards for implementation in practice, for industrial production."[3]

The guiding role, which Gropius had intended for the skilled trades, was largely assumed by industry and engineers, who found their partners and areas for experimentation among innovative architects, enlightened clients and authorities. The construction process was optimized through the rational (pre-)fabrication of semi-finished products and through the use of construction machines and assembly methods. Cranes, conveyer belts and spray- or injection rendering machines began to dominate the scene on the building site. As the building tasks and building processes underwent an evolution in the first half of the 20th century, the training and professional profile of architects and engineers also changed. Specialization became more common. By the end of the 1920s it was already common practice that structural engineers collaborated as essential partners with architects in planning not only engineered structures, but all construction: load-bearing structures of great span width or great height, optimized both in terms of material and systems, could only be realized with verifiable structural calculations and tests, including the structural joining compounds. In addition to planning, production and execution, a new sector emerged in the industry, the building authority with special building laws, standards, state examination and site supervision. Production and assembly processes are not tied to any particular architectural style. A department store design in a classicistic style could be erected as an iron skeleton structure just as easily as the department stores designed by Erich Mendelsohn in Wroclaw or Stuttgart. However, it is entirely justified to describe the classic modern as the most rigorous translation of industrialization, which is continuing to this day. Once again, the evolution in building

4.2

4.3

and especially energy technologies will change the houses of the future in much the same way as earlier innovations did some eighty years ago. Innovation, skill and industrialization have made the adaptable, flexible and climate-adjusted house a reality. The prognosis of many architects from the modern era that entire houses would one day be mass-produced like industrial products on an assembly line – comparable to car manufacture – has not come true, however. Despite numerous attempts, the concept has remained utopian.

Renovation and preservation

Heritage protected buildings from the modern era, realized with concepts, materials and industrially manufactured parts of prefabricated components that were new at the time, present architects, engineers, conservators, restorers and craftsmen with extremely complex and difficult tasks.
In looking at a building, our perception is focused on the surfaces, which form bodies, areas and interior spaces. Elements such as walls, columns, ceilings, roofs, windows, doors, technical appliances, installations or interior fittings are made of materials fundamentally defined by their material properties and manufacturing processes, in addition to their architectural and functional design, e.g., thin iron window casements. Structures can display the material from which they are constructed as surface – for example, brick in exposed or fair-faced brickwork – or hide it behind plaster, coatings or panels with yet another wide range of material properties. The Einstein Tower by Erich Mendelsohn serves as a document that not all attempts in the early phase of modernism successfully translated building design into fitting structural uses of material: the curved forms of the tower consist of a plastered mixed structure composed of masonry and reinforced concrete (Fig. 4.2). Even experienced experts must rely upon insights from building research, building i.e. construction history and last but not least detail studies at the building and in laboratories, in order to recognize the construction of building component and load-bearing structure and the various mechanical and physical forces. Especially in cases where building materials and systems were used, which were briefly available in great variety after the mid-19th century and then quickly fell into disuse or were further developed. Cataloguing and describing damages, including earlier repairs, is another important step in renovation planning. Differentiated analyses of the causes of these damages are indispensable, addressing in particular:
• Aging, material fatigue and wear and tear,
• poor/non-existent maintenance and upkeep,
• inexpert repairs and renovations,
• user behavior in terms of heating and cooling,
• the status of the building technology and standards of the time,
• and planning or production errors.

Renovation planning thus always begins with intensive studies of what exists, what has been altered and also what has been lost. No matter how carefully these tasks are

4.1   Bauhaus building in Dessau, Walter Gropius (1926)
4.2   Einstein Tower, Erich Mendelsohn (1921)
4.3   Employment office, Walter Gropius in Dessau (1929)

4.4

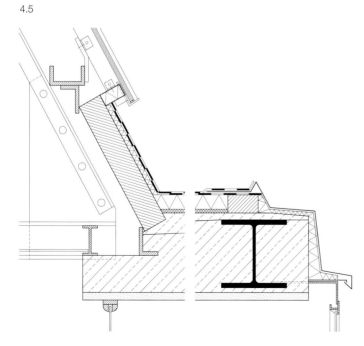

4.5

approached, new and old damages can resurface even after the renovation due to the original construction. Basement walls of buildings with only partial basements cannot be properly insulated after the fact, cracked xylolite (stonewood) floors or corroded iron sections – in masonry or encased in concrete – cannot be completely repaired for the long term; the building remains a "chronic patient". Preservation of the original substance of the monument as far as possible is preferable to a complete renewal, and clients, executing firms and conservation authorities must collaborate to find solutions for each individual case. After fifty to seventy years it is unavoidable that many building components and interior fittings are irrevocably worn out. In traditional constructions with wood or stone it is usually possible to undertake repairs that are true to the original material and manufacture or even to replace damaged parts. Typified parts such as window sections and fixtures, ceiling systems, glass components, but also technical elements such as heating units or floor coverings, on the other hand, are usually irreplaceable. They are no longer available or no longer satisfy contemporary standards i.e. relevant norms; manufacturers have closed down, products were changed, or are no longer on the market for technical or aesthetic reasons. Building system components such as pipes, wiring, central warm water heating – the latest innovation in the 1920s – must today be classified as unfit for repair or maintenance. Installations for communication media are non-existent. Architects renovating buildings with valuable surfaces are faced with nearly unsolvable challenges arising from this set of problems. In response to rising demands, small firms have in the meantime filled a gap in the market by reproducing limited editions of individual products. This is hardly possible, however, for articles such as wire glass or figured glass, iron casement sections or linoleum in some colours, which can only be produced in large volumes with elaborate machine input. In these cases, one is forced to resort to technologically and aesthetically compatible new products. Some "classic" 1920s and 1930s products are still or once again on the market. These include the so-called Gropius door handle and the Wagenfeld lamp, as well as a solid brown linoleum. Plaster and colours are either still available in unchanged historical composition or can be remixed.

A case study: the former employment office in Dessau by Walter Gropius (1929)

The employment office in Dessau, for which the chief architect of Berlin, Martin Wagner, provided the functional description in 1925, was a completely new building type in its day. Gropius's studio was awarded the commission for the new construction in a competition. The building consists of a round structure for the public, a two-story administration wing and a stairwell, which provides the visual focus of the building (Fig. 4.3). By order of the city of Dessau, the former employment office was completely renovated from 2000 to 2003.

The skeleton
Although concrete and reinforced concrete were tried and tested building materials in the 1920s, they are rarely found as primary structural systems in the early modern buildings in Germany, with the exception of foundations, basement walls and to some degree cantilevered ceilings or stairs.

Examples of well-known reinforced concrete constructions from the modern era are the Bauhaus building from 1926, also by Gropius, and the hat factory in Luckenwalde, erected in 1922 by Erich Mendelsohn with its filigree reinforced concrete frames. It is often overlooked that the development and realization of modern iron and reinforced concrete structures were frequently achieved thanks to engineers like Finsterwalder and Maillart, and contractors like Züblin or Dyckerhoff & Widmann and others. In the case of Gropius's employment office, the primary load-bearing structure consists of partially bent iron sections, the iron skeleton, calculated and executed by the wagon factory at Dessau. This ensured a time efficient and economical construction process. In iron skeleton structures, all interior and exterior walls and columns must be infilled or clad. In the case of the employment office, as by the way in his earliest modern building, the Fagus factory in Alfeld/Leine (1911–1914), Gropius opted for fair-faced brickwork with yellow clinker bricks. This correct and sensible construction method of a steel skeleton enclosed in masonry is, however, subject to the risk of hidden corrosion, when rainwater or moisture penetrate to the iron girders as a result of poor maintenance or structural changes. Detailed studies of the brickwork of the employment office showed that the iron girders, originally coated in red lead, were severely corroded due to open, water-permeable joints and leaks in the ceilings. No evidence was found of humidity penetrating into the walls from the inside, the result of subsequent sanitary installations or windows that are sealed too tight. It was therefore not necessary to strip the structure down to the girders, which would have meant a substantial loss of structure.

Since the end of the 19th century, the market was flooded with countless massive ceiling systems in a variety of executions – from in-situ concrete to prefabricated stone and brick elements in combination with iron girders and rebars. The so-called Kleine ceiling, first introduced in 1892, which was used in the employment office in Dessau, was a siderite ceiling manufactured from light bricks, which dominated the market for a long time. In addition to structural and economic advantages, this ceiling construction also offered improved fire protection. A flat roof seemed the only alternative for the employment office in Dessau because of the part round, part cubic shape of the fabric. This saved it from the fate of Gropius's master residences in Dessau, which were "aryanized" with gable roofs during the Third Reich. The flat roof of the round building with internal drainage features three semi-circular iron-framework sheds, which provide natural lighting as well as ventilation and extraction for the interior. The renovation created an entirely new flat roof structure with foamglass as insulation (Fig. 4.5). The insulation layer was reduced along the edge of the flat roof to preserve the historic details of the sheet lining in the original scale. [4] The shed glazing with single wire glass panes was also left unchanged, although the internal horizontal light skylight was restored with insulated glass.

The completion
At the time when the employment office was built, plaster, paint and wallpaper, terrazzo, screed or xylolite floors were already being industrially manufactured and then installed on site; machines were commonly used for these processes.

Among the products, which characterized the completion of the employment office, were the windows with the typified casements and fittings, as well as the terrazzo and xylolite floor coverings, which alternated with wood floors in the interior. Since the restorers were unable to fully reconstruct all surfaces, only those rooms were restored to their original condition where sufficient material had been preserved. Original remnants can be preserved, for example, with the help of reversible mackled wallpapers or coatings. The fundamental demand of new building to bring light and sun into buildings and thus to respond flexibly to sunshine and warm or cold temperatures, led to a completely new window technology. The architect could choose from a wide range of glasses, from single-pane transparent window glass, to carved or etched ornamental cast glass, to glass bricks or concrete glass bricks, which allowed light to penetrate through massive ceilings. The round structure contains a skylight with prismatic glass, which was very popular in the 1920s and especially recreated for the employment office. Light is evenly distributed throughout the interior by means of deflection. Prismatic glass of this kind has been unavailable for some time. By chance, a search led to remaining stock of such panes in Spain. More than 1 500 pieces, reconfigured as insulated laminated panes, were placed loosely into partially reinforced iron frames composed of T- and L-sections (Fig. 4.6). Special permission is required to process prismatic cast glass into insulated laminated panes, especially when it is used for overhead glazing.

Building physics and climate
Large glass surfaces and single-pane windows generally provide the initial impetus to think about the physics of the materials and components, and also about the climate responses of a building. As for the structure and the completion, it is important to take stock of the existing components and to evaluate them as a basis for the renovation planning that follows. In the case of the employment office in Dessau, as in most other buildings of the classic modern, the existing insulation does not conform to current minimum requirements. The climate concept of the time can nevertheless be regarded as logical in its own right. When the insulation is changed and improved – provided that such modifications are possible in the context of heritage protection – it is important to ensure that heating and ventilation, sanitation and even future uses are compatible with the original insulation. A reversal of weak areas, e.g. replacing single-glazed and relatively leaky windows with insulated glazing without additional measures, usually changes the original climate concept of the structure, which can lead to considerable damage on and in the building. The skylights and large windows of the employment office are constructed in continuous steel frames, that is, without thermal buffers, with ventilation wings and condensation gutters. To improve insulation, increase comfort and decrease running costs, the original single glazing was preserved, but a second layer was added behind it to form a kind of box-type window. The same approach was employed for the wood-frame windows set into the external walls of the round building in 1936. The attention given to a functioning ventilation and climate-control system is demonstrated by a ventilation

4.4   Renovation of the shed roof
4.5   Roof edge and connection to shed glazing

33

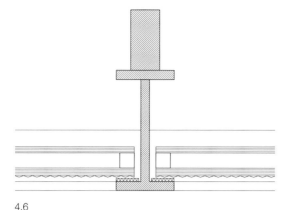

4.6

network composed of pipes, ducts and hollow columns, which supported natural ventilation in the building with the help of a Junkers fan and mechanical ventilation flaps, and which has been re-activated after the renovation.

The interior
Architects of the modern era took a far more comprehensive approach to the building and its interior than is common today. They designed the furniture and lighting for the new interior spaces and uses of the time. The cupboard can serve as a perfect example to illustrate the relationship between space, function and design: every opportunity was used to construct cupboards as interior walls, room dividers or beneath stairs; the free-standing cupboard became a thing of the past, or rather, it was integrated into the structure. The technical achievements of the industrial age, such as warm water, running cold and hot water, artificial light, electrical appliances, functional and modern kitchens, became indispensable components of the modern building. There was much experimentation with artificial and natural light to achieve optimum general or zonal lighting. Aside from the manufacturers, architects, designers and engineers, and finally an entire department of the Bauhaus in Dessau, dedicated their energies to developing new lighting systems. While most of these luminaires and lamps had the appearance of industrial products, they were generally handcrafted, albeit with the help of semi-finished goods such as metal tubes and glasses. The employment office in Dessau featured prototype spherical lamps in the circulation areas, which are still in use today. Because the luminance they provided was insufficient, they had to be complemented with modern spotlights set above the luminous ceiling. The work areas, on the other hand, have been equipped with modern luminaires. However, when the lighting is set accordingly, visitors can still experience in the corridors how low the interior lighting was seventy years ago.

Endangered and destroyed buildings
After 1933, the National Socialists had issued a demolition order for the employment office in Dessau designed by Walter Gropius. In the end, the building was rescued by the chaos of war and the building shortage in the city. Despite poor maintenance, more than 90 per cent of the original substance remains intact. Today, the building is once again home to a public office, the road traffic authorities of Dessau. There, visitors are able to not only present their concerns, they can also experience a piece of modern architectural history.

It would be a mistake to assume that valuable buildings from the classic era of Modernism or postwar Modernism are safe from demolition as a result of heritage protection. Demolition orders are currently tabled for the Faber high-rise in Magdeburg (1930), one of the first high-rises in the print-media sector, for the Hochtief administration building in Frankfurt (1966), a major work by Egon Eiermann, for the Blumlägerfeld housing complex, completed in 1930 by Otto Haesler with its distinctive minimum-cost housing. Other buildings, such as the Land War Pension Office by the brothers Luckhardt in Munich (1953–1989) or Jörg Schlaich's cable-guyed cooling tower (1974–1991), have already been destroyed. Commercial interests prevail over heritage protection and the public mandate to preserve important cultural assets.

Conversely, some people believe that destroyed buildings can be brought back to life through so-called reconstructions, as if the destruction had never happened. Examples are the master residences by Gropius in Dessau, the Universitätskirche in Leipzig and, last but not least, the castles in Potsdam, Berlin or Braunschweig. If we consider a building as part of our cultural heritage, then an imitation of questionable provenance, with new materials and without the traces of history simply cannot replace the task and legacy of a monument.

Conclusion

Fortunately many buildings and neighborhoods from the modern era are still preserved and in use. The international association DOCOMOMO, which currently has 35 member countries, documents the monuments of the era, engages in dialogue on the architectural theories they represent and seeks to develop technical solutions for renovation and preservation. Like never before in the history of building and technology, buildings from the modern era – highly delicate constructs – require a comprehensive study of the interaction between architecture, function, structure and building climate prior to renovation. Long-forgotten technologies and ideas can provide valuable insights for contemporary planning and current user behavior. The buildings of the modern era and the renovation initiatives can serve as exemplary case studies for a comprehensive approach to new construction and for the widespread renovation efforts that will soon be required for the buildings erected in the past fifty years.

Notes:
1   Gropius, Walter: Das flache Dach. Internationale Umfrage über die technische Durchführbarkeit horizontal abgedeckter Dächer und Balkone. In: Bauwelt 9/1926
2   Deutscher Werkbund (ed.): Bau und Wohnung. Stuttgart 1927
3   Argan, Gulio Carlo: Gropius und das Bauhaus. Hamburg 1962 and: Nerdinger, Winfried: Der Architekt Walter Gropius. Berlin 1996
4   40 mm thick foamglass panels were laid onto hot asphalt across the entire flat roof of the round building. 60 mm strong foamglass panels were installed in the shed roof area to optimize insulation.

Bibliography:
1   Burkhardt, B.(ed.): Baudenkmale der Moderne, Geschichte einer Instandsetzung: Scharoun, Haus Schminke. Stuttgart 2002
2   Burkhardt, B.; Weber, C.: Das Arbeitsamtsgebäude von Walter Gropius in Dessau (1929–1999). In: Stadtarchiv Dessau (ed.): Dessauer Kalender, 44th edition, Dessau 2000
3   Gebeßler, A. (ed.): Baudenkmale der Moderne, Geschichte einer Instandsetzung: Gropius, Meisterhaus Muche/Schlemmer. Stuttgart 2003
4   Graupner, K.; Lobers, F.: Bauklimatische Aspekte, Heizungs- und Lüftungskonzept. In: Burkhardt, B. (ed.): Baudenkmal der Moderne, Geschichte einer Instandsetzung: Scharoun, Haus Schminke. Stuttgart 2002
5   Huse, N. (ed.): Baudenkmale der Moderne, Geschichte einer Instandsetzung: Mendelsohn, der Einsteinturm. Stuttgart 2000
6   Kirsch, K.: Werkbund exhibition "Die Wohnung", Stuttgart 1927, Die Weißenhofsiedlung, catalogue. Stuttgart 1992
7   Klapheck, R.: Gussglas. Düsseldorf 1938
8   Pauser, A.: Eisenbeton 1850–1950.Vienna 1994
9   Rasch, H.und B.: Wie Bauen? 2 volumes. Stuttgart 1927
10   Schulze, K.W.: Der Stahlskelettbau. Stuttgart 1928
11   Siedler, E.J.: Die Lehre vom neuen Bauen. Ein Handbuch der Baustoffe und Bauweisen. Berlin 1932
12   Stephan, R.: Erich Mendelsohn – Dynamics and Function, exhibition catalogue of the Institute for International Relations Stuttgart. Stuttgart 1998

4.6   Vertical section of luminous ceiling in employment office
4.7   Circulation zone in round building after renovation

4.7

Project: heritage renovation of the former employment office in Dessau; conversion into road traffic authority of the city of Dressau
Client: the city of Dessau, Hochbauamt
Architect: Bauatelier Walter Gropius Dessau/Berlin
Year: 1928–1929, Renovation: 2000–2003
Conversion and renovation, historic studies:
Burkhardt + Schumacher, Architects and engineers, Braunschweig
Associate: Joachim Tappe
Restoration: Restauratorenkollektiv Pröpper + Hänel, Blankenburg
Conservation: Untere Denkmalschutzbehörde Dessau, Landesamt für Denkmalpflege Sachsen-Anhalt, Halle/Saale

The Projects

Urban Renewal in Salemi

Architect: Álvaro Siza Vieira, Oporto,
Roberto Collovà, Palermo

In 1968, an earthquake shook western Sicily, destroying much of the town of Salemi. After years of administrative and political wrangling, the architects succeeded in implementing their scheme for the reorganization of the public urban spaces. Construction work began in 1982 at various points in the old town centre. With the design of a network of routes and the creation of new links in the form of stairs and alleyways, the structure of the town has been transformed.

The architects proposed a wide range of measures, from the use of various types of paving to the installation of new street lamps and balustrades of unified design.

The centrepiece of the project is the main town square, situated on the crest of the hill where Arabs founded the original settlement. The square is flanked by the ruins of the cathedral, by a castle that once belonged to a Swabian knight, and by two- to three-storey terraced housing.

The church, which was destroyed in the earthquake, was not rebuilt. Its ruins have now been minimally refurbished and incorporated into the public open space to form a new focus of urban life. The raised platform of the cathedral has been covered with white stone from the nearby town of Trapani, and stone blocks mark the positions of the former columns, a couple of which have been re-erected. Rather like a stage set, the ruined walls of the apse now define one end of the square. From here, narrow lanes cut their way through the dense urban fabric, leading to further squares and courtyards with new shops and facilities.

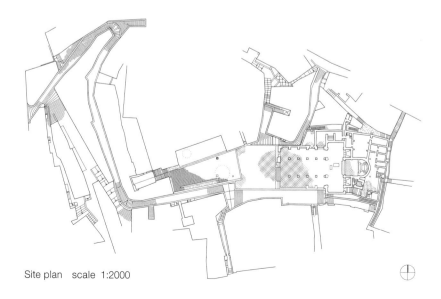

Site plan   scale 1:2000

39

39

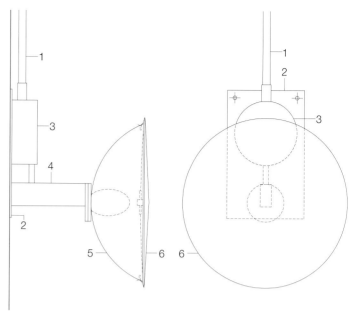

Light fitting   scale 1:10

1 stainless-steel cable conduit
2 5 mm stainless-steel plate
3 Ø 170 mm junction box
4 30/60 mm stainless-steel RHS
5 Ø 450 mm perspex casing
6 Ø 450 mm stainless-steel cover

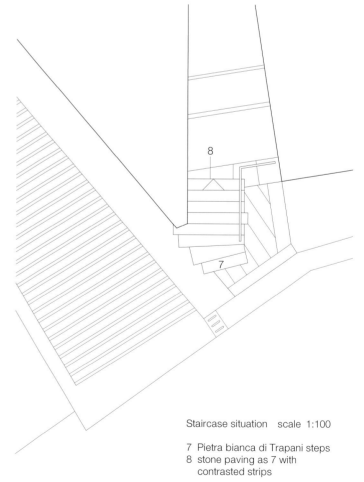

Staircase situation   scale 1:100

7 Pietra bianca di Trapani steps
8 stone paving as 7 with
   contrasted strips

40

Cultural Centre in Toledo

Architect: Ignacio Mendaro Corsini, Madrid

The former church of San Marco, squeezed into the historic district of Toledo on what was once a monastery site at the highest point of the city, stood unused for many years. Following a national architectural ideas competition, a civic archive with seminar rooms was created on the site, while the church itself has been converted into a cultural centre. Historic remains that reveal early Christian, Jewish and Islamic influences in this former royal city have been carefully integrated into the new complex.

The monastery was founded in 1220, later destroyed, and subsequently rebuilt in the middle of the 16th century. The church, which belonged to the Trinitarian order, dates from the 17th and 18th centuries and is a typical ecclesiastical structure of its time, an example of early Baroque Spanish architecture. After the process of secularization, the buildings served as a military base and were again destroyed in 1960. The church remained for a few more years in the hands of the Trinitarians, but in 1980, the entire complex was acquired by the government.

After securing the ruins and consolidating the subsoil and foundations, the interior of the church and the facades that had been exposed after the demolition of the monastery were restored. Despite the treatment to which the facades were subjected, the image of a church remains. The nave has been transformed into an auditorium with fixed seating, while the two aisles are used for exhibitions. The archives are located one floor below, half buried in the ground. From a distance, the ten-metre-high walls enclosing the archives lend the church the appearance of a fortified structure. The closed concrete facade, which aroused a storm of protest in this traditionally minded city, has a warm golden coloration that matches the surrounding urban fabric. Visitors enter the complex through a tall, wide opening. The concrete floor slab within is raised above Roman and medieval excavations, allowing a view of these tokens of the past. Visitors enter the civic archives on the gallery floors, from where one can look down to the reading room below. Daylight enters the tall space in a controlled form via roof lights and small openings, evoking a mystical, almost monastic atmosphere within. Sections of the steel shuttering to the concrete structure were left in position to form the window surrounds.

With simple, restrained means, the new architecture has been carefully integrated into the existing fabric. Old and new are nevertheless distinguished through the choice of materials.

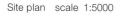

Site plan   scale 1:5000

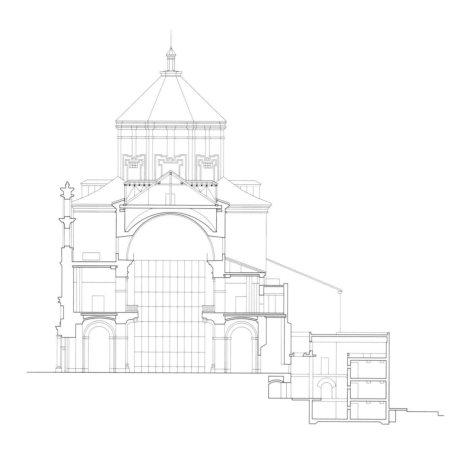

Section
Plan at hall level
Plan at archive
entrance level
scale 1:500

1 Entrance to hall
2 Hall
3 Small hall
4 Archives
5 Access to archive
  courtyard
6 Courtyard
7 Entrance to archives
8 Void over
  reading room
9 Administration
10 Kiosk

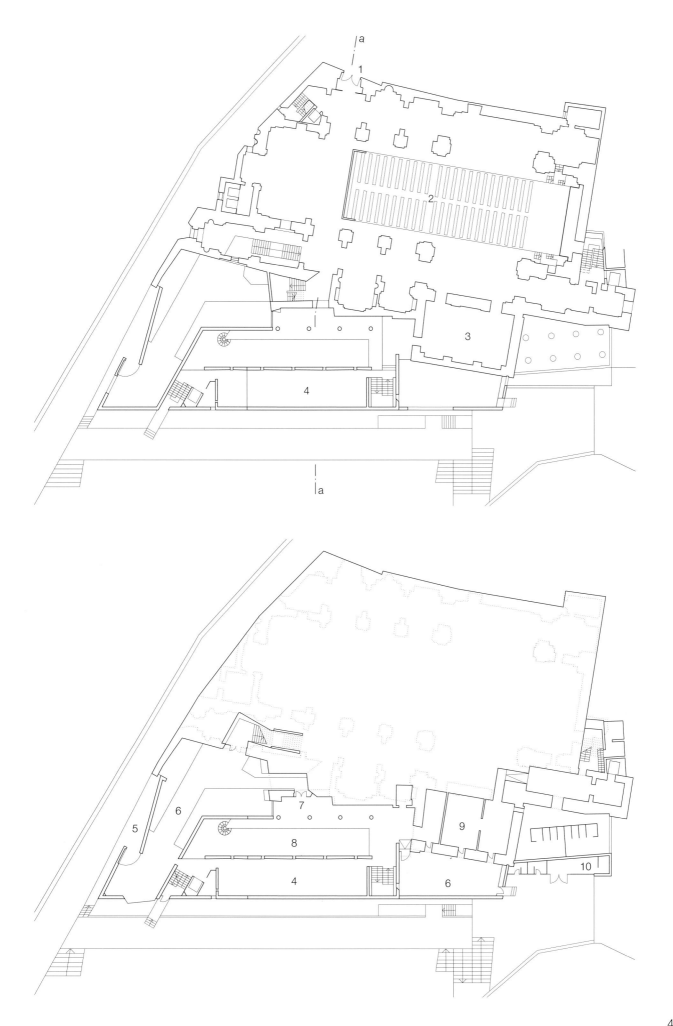

Window details
scale 1:10
scale 1:2.5

1 10 mm oxidized,
   polished and
   varnished sheet-steel
   permanant shuttering
   as window surround
2 Ø 10 mm steel rod
3 40/6 mm steel flat
4 10/10 mm steel SHS
5 12 mm laminated safety glass
6 Ø 5 mm openings for ventilation
7 shadow joint
8 steel anchor
9 60 mm steel T-section
10 Ø 50 mm opening
   for compacting concrete

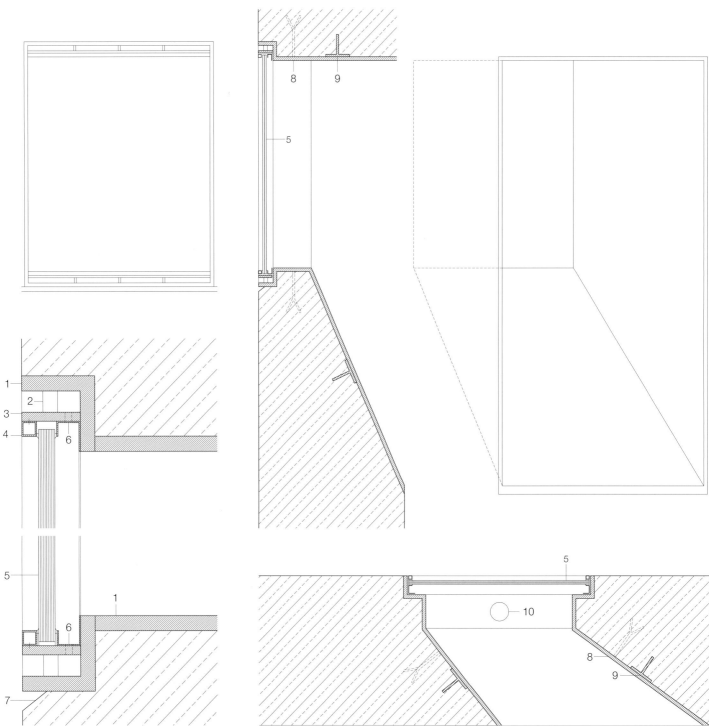

Sections · Plan   scale 1:100
Cross-section through bridge   scale 1:20

1 100/50 mm steel RHS
2 4 mm oxidized, polished and
   varnished sheet steel
3 100 mm rigid-foam insulation between
   100/50 mm steel RHSs
4 fluorescent tube
5 perforated removable covering
6 30 mm parquet
   30 mm composite wood board
   50 mm insulation between
   50/50 mm steel SHSs
   80 mm insulation between
   50/80 mm steel RHSs
   4 mm sheet steel
7 50/50 steel SHS
8 steel-flat skirting strip

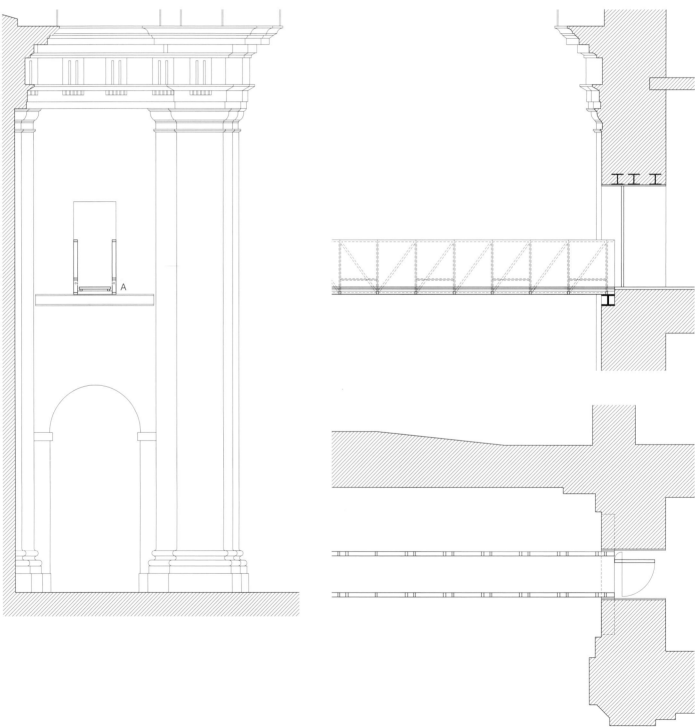

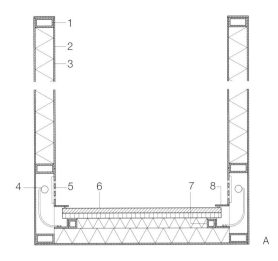

1
2
3

4 5 6 7 8 A

Museum in Colmenar Viejo

Architects: Aranguren Gallegos, Madrid

In 1722, the priest in Colmenar Viejo, a town north of Madrid, founded a school for Latin and classical studies. It was built in a traditional style typical of the region. Adjoining the main building was an extension with a press, where wine was produced and stored. The entire Casa del Maestro Almeida complex, as it is known, is of great historical significance in the town. The city of Madrid, therefore, commissioned the architects to refurbish the old wine-press structure and to convert it to a new use. The other sections of the building are to be restored at a later date. The former wine-press tract has now been transformed into a small museum in which the traditional wine production process is explained and illustrated. The building is concealed behind the former school at the centre of the town. The materials used in the construction – stone and pre-oxidized steel – match the historical surroundings, and at first sight, the refurbishment work is scarcely distinguishable from the existing fabric. The new materials nevertheless stand out in their form and in the way they are used as independent elements.

From the road, one passes through a gateway in the wall and enters a courtyard. The gate consists of four concrete slabs of different sizes enclosed in steel frames. In the courtyard, large precast concrete paving slabs with open reinforcing loops were laid loose on a bed of gravel so that they can be easily removed when the main building is refurbished at a later date. The garden is enclosed with tall vertical metal sheeting.

It was possible to retain only the walls of the original extension structure; the roof had already fallen in. Internally, the floor has been finished with clay brick tiles. The brick walls have been cleaned, repaired and rebuilt to a greater height in part. Externally, the facades are clad with lapped beige-grey granite slabs. Since it was not possible to determine the load-bearing capacity of the walls, steel columns were erected to support the pitched roof, which now consists of laminated timber structural members with an internal wood lining. Externally, the edge of the roof is covered with natural coloured zinc sheeting with a matt lead-oxide coating. At the top of the walls, windows with industrial glass allow daylight to enter, providing subdued lighting in the exhibition space.

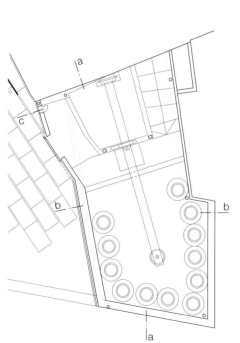

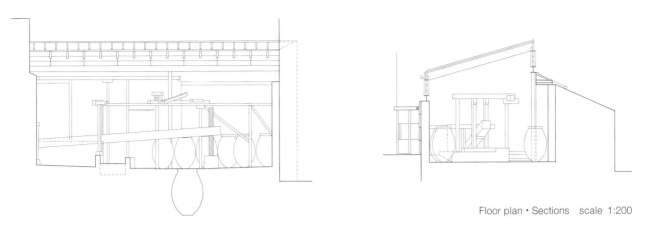

Floor plan · Sections   scale 1:200

Section
scale 1:20

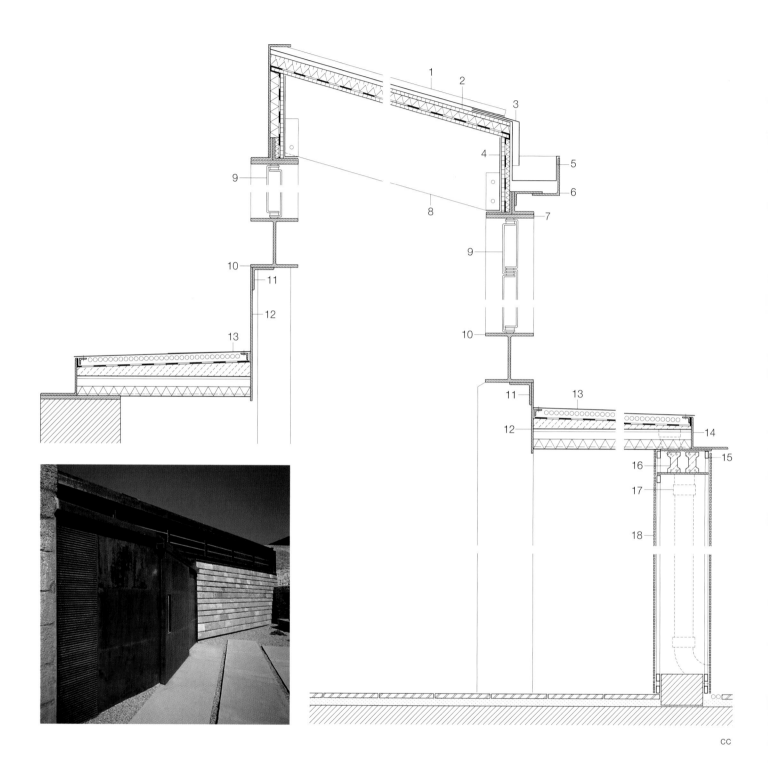

cc

1 sheet-zinc standing-seam roofing
2 sandwich panel:
   18 mm phenolic-resin-coated composite wood board
   40 mm extruded polystyrene thermal insulation, vapour barrier
   18 mm phenolic-resin-coated composite wood board
3 5 mm pre-oxidized-steel sheeting
4 5 mm pre-oxidized-steel sheeting phenolic-resin-coated composite wood board

   vapour barrier
   extruded polystyrene thermal insulation
5 double sheet-zinc rainwater gutter to falls
6 200/150/10 mm pre-oxidized steel angle
7 20 mm pre-oxidized steel plate
8 100/400 mm laminated timber beam
9 ⊔-section glass elements sealed with

   30/3 mm silicone strips
10 pre-oxidized steel I-beam 260 mm deep
11 120/120/12 mm pre-oxidized steel angle
12 10 mm pre-oxidized steel plate
13 roof construction:
   pre-oxidized sheet-steel roofing
   layer of gravel
   bituminous sealing layer
   lightweight concrete finished to falls

   4 mm galvanized steel sheeting
   steel I-beams 100 mm deep
   50 mm polyurethane rigid-foam insulation
   5 mm pre-oxidized sheet steel
14 200/200 mm pre-oxidized steel angle
15 20/40 mm steel RHS
16 precast concrete lintel
17 rainwater pipe
18 pre-oxidized steel ventilation louvres

Shop Entrance in New York

Architects: Future Systems, London

West Chelsea, once a run-down district of New York with derelict warehouses, has been turned into an upmarket area. Reasonable rents attracted a lot of young artists, and in the meantime, the individual environment they created has become a fitting setting for a wide range of galleries, clubs, restaurants and fashion boutiques. In collaboration with the architects, the Japanese fashion designer Rei Kawakubo developed a new concept for her brand name, "Comme des Garçons". Her aim was to create an artistic ambience for her unusual clothing design in various locations. A dilapidated 19th-century red-brick facade is the dominant outward feature of the building in which her new shop is located. There are no display windows in which to present her fashion to passers-by in the street. The boutique lies concealed between art galleries, and, like the works they present, her clothing is not intended for public display. It has to be discovered.

The facade was left unchanged – with its old signs and an external fire-escape ladder. Leading from the entrance portal into the interior, a tunnel-like, asymmetric tubular structure forms a transition between the existing building and the newly designed shop space, where the clothing is set off against a series of sculpturally shaped walls. Visitors pass from the bustle of the street through the slightly constricted neck of the tube into the calmer atmosphere of the boutique. The glass entrance door at the outer end affords a glimpse of the interior. The tube was constructed with metal sheeting of adequate thickness to make it self-supporting and self-bracing. It is divided into five segments and requires no supporting structure. The three-dimensionally curved sheet-metal sections were manufactured in an English shipyard, transported to New York and assembled on site.

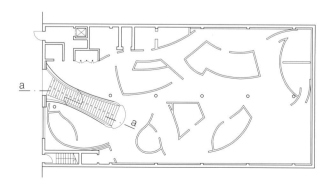

Floor plan   scale 1:400
Axonometric of entrance

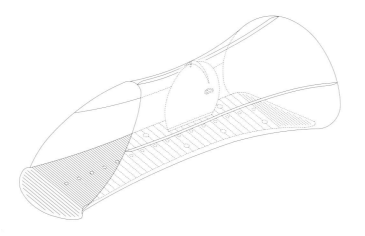

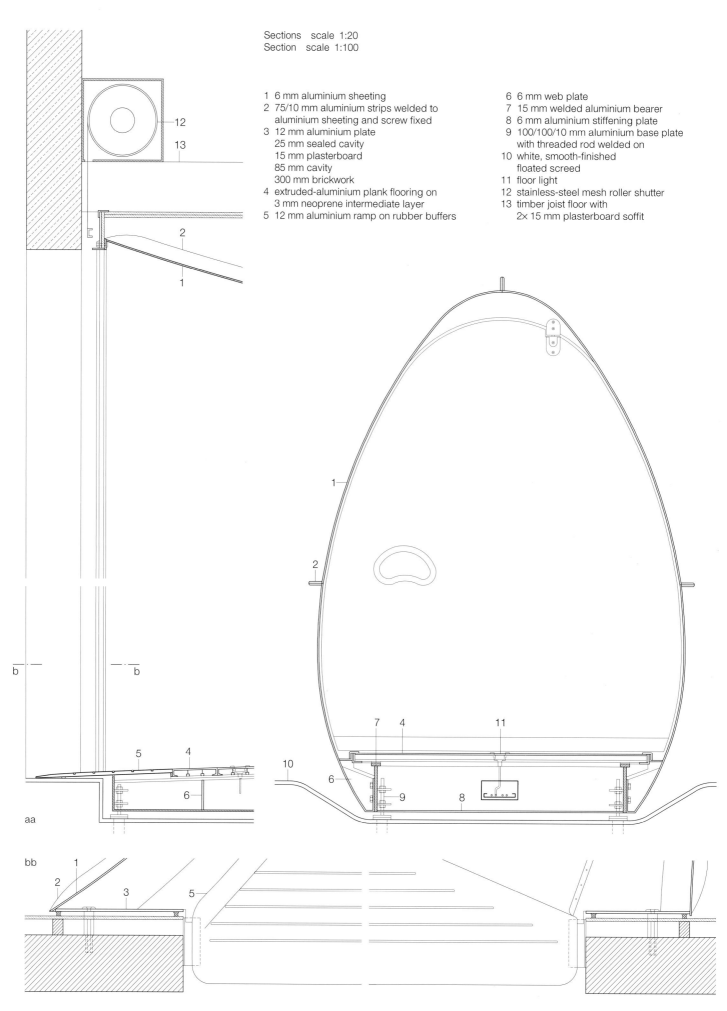

Sections scale 1:20
Section scale 1:100

1 6 mm aluminium sheeting
2 75/10 mm aluminium strips welded to
   aluminium sheeting and screw fixed
3 12 mm aluminium plate
   25 mm sealed cavity
   15 mm plasterboard
   85 mm cavity
   300 mm brickwork
4 extruded-aluminium plank flooring on
   3 mm neoprene intermediate layer
5 12 mm aluminium ramp on rubber buffers

6 6 mm web plate
7 15 mm welded aluminium bearer
8 6 mm aluminium stiffening plate
9 100/100/10 mm aluminium base plate
   with threaded rod welded on
10 white, smooth-finished
   floated screed
11 floor light
12 stainless-steel mesh roller shutter
13 timber joist floor with
   2× 15 mm plasterboard soffit

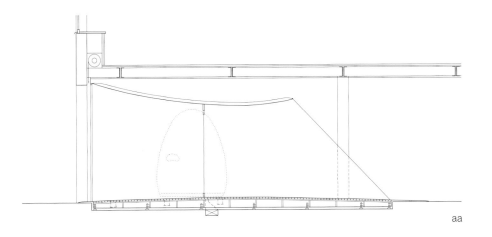

aa

Visitors' Centre in Criewen

Architects: Anderhalten Architects, Berlin

Criewen Palace in Brandenburg, Germany, stands in the middle of a landscaped park designed by Peter Joseph Lenné. In the course of its conversion into a German-Polish meeting place, the former sheep house has been turned into an information centre for visitors. Erected in 1820 and later raised in height for the purpose of drying tobacco, the building was neglected for a long time and ultimately fell into a state of dilapidation. In refurbishing it for its new use, the entire internal timber construction and the roof had to be removed. Since dampness in the brickwork had reduced the load-bearing capacity of the walls, the architects inserted a new steel structure, leaving a 60 cm space around the building between the steel columns and the inner faces of the external walls. The walls were also left exposed, which facilitates the drying out process and allows the brickwork to be kept under observation. One of the most striking features of the construction is the 45-metre-long wattle facade screen, which provides protection against driving rain and serves as a light filter. Originally used in dyke-building in the polders along the River Oder, this material is well integrated in the new facade design. Access to the information centre is via three draught-excluding lobbies inserted in the entrance front. The exhibition area consists of a wood deck raised above the former barn floor. The linear character of the hall is accentuated by the slender new roof purlins, between which radiant heating panels have been installed to warm the space beneath. The new double-glazed windows inserted at the upper level behind the existing wood-louvre fascia are not visible from the outside. The former barn windows on the lower floor have been left with single glazing. As the weakest point of the structure in terms of building physics, they have an indicator function: if condensation develops, the humidity can be regulated via ventilation elements in the louvre zone at the top of the facade.

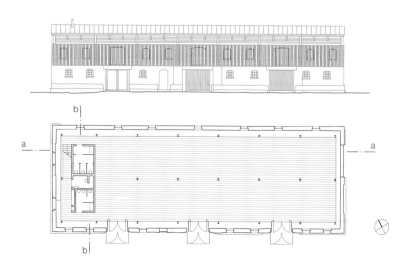

Elevation · Floor plan
scale 1:500

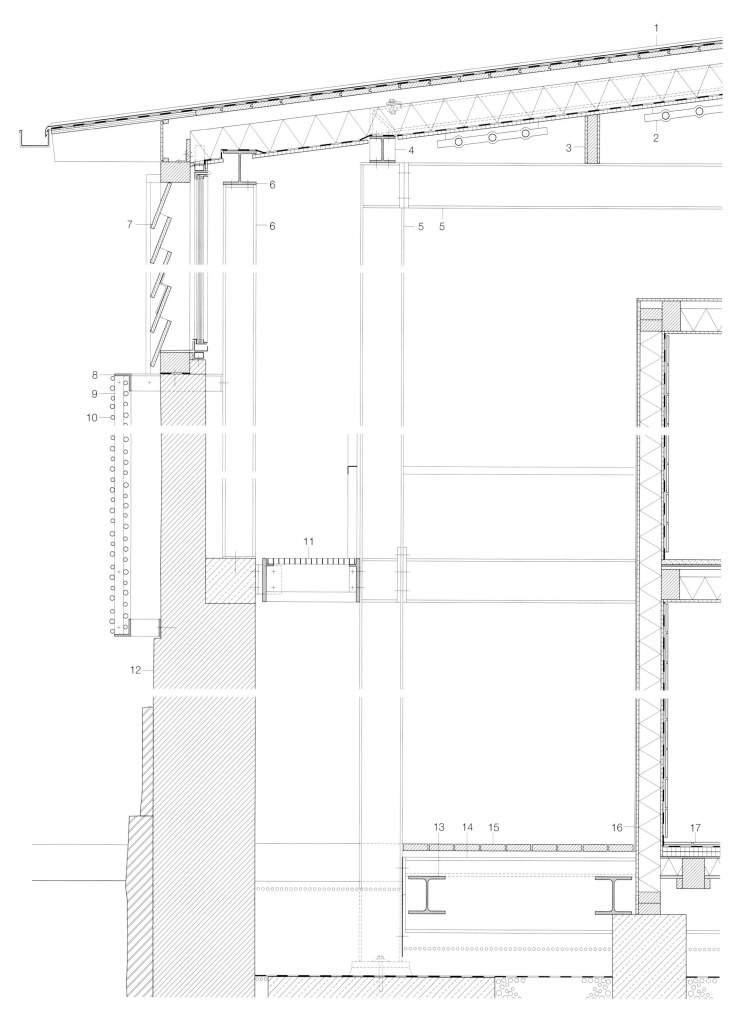

1

2

3

4

6

6

5 5

7

8

9

10

11

12

13 14 15

16

17

60

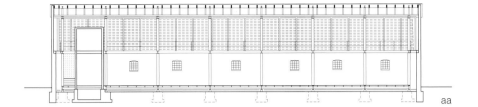

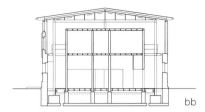

aa   bb

Sectional details
scale 1:20
Longitudinal section
Cross-section
scale 1:400

1 roof construction:
   sheet-zinc roofing
   bituminous sealing layer
   28 mm sawn softwood tongued-and-
   grooved boarding
   160/240 mm timber rafters
   160 mm mineral-fibre insulation
   sheet-polythene vapour barrier
   18 mm beech-veneered plywood
2 radiant heating panel
3 80 mm purlins lined with veneered plywood
4 steel I-beam 140 mm deep
5 steel I-beam/column 240 mm deep
6 steel I-beam/column 180 mm deep
7 existing wood louvres
8 90/90/9 mm steel angle frame
9 50/10 mm steel flat
10 wattle screen consisting of willow osiers
11 peripheral metal grating (30/90 mm mesh)
12 existing brick wall
13 secondary steel I-beam 200 mm deep
14 main steel I-beam 400 mm deep
15 135/50 mm white oak boarding
16 wall construction to sanitary cell:
   6 mm fibre-cement sheeting on
   13 mm chipboard
   120 mm mineral-fibre thermal insulation
   water-resistant compressed board
   with sealing coat
   11 mm stoneware tiles, adhesive fixed
17 floor construction in sanitary cell:
   11 mm stoneware tiles, adhesive fixed
   sealing layer
   2× 25 mm composite wood board
   10 mm impact-sound insulating mat
   120/160 mm timber beams
   thermal insulation between beams
   16 mm composite wood board on
   wood bearers

Entrance details
scale 1:20

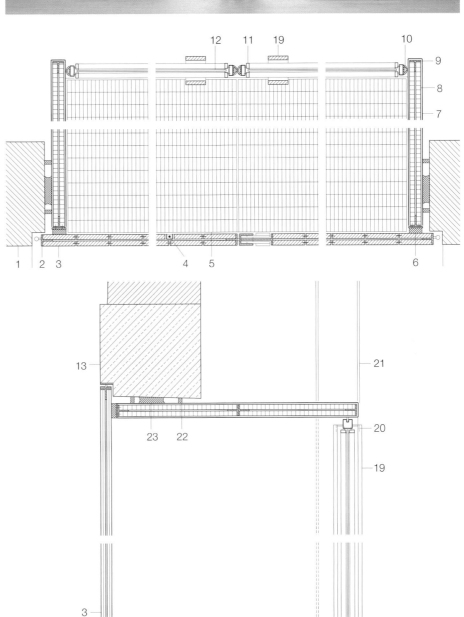

1 existing brick wall
2 60/45/5 mm steel T-section frame
3 178/26 mm white oak cross-tongued
   boarding
4 fixing bolt in 30/30/3 mm steel channel
5 steel grating (22.2/66.6 mm mesh) on
   30/20 mm hard-rubber bearers
6 neoprene sealing strip
7 3 mm sheet-steel lining
8 24 mm composite wood board
9 60/60/7 mm steel T-section
10 cellular sealing strip on 50/25/3 mm
   aluminium RHS
11 30/15 mm steel glazing bead
12 8 mm toughened safety glass
13 reinforced concrete lintel
14 exposed concrete apron slab with
   roughened non-slip surface
15 6/55 mm steel flat
16 drainage
17 50/50/4 mm steel SHS with brush seal
18 110/60/8 mm welded steel channel section
19 20/110 mm white oak door push
20 35/35/3 mm steel angle fixing bracket
21 steel I-section column 240 mm deep
22 20 mm foam-rubber gasket
23 extruded polystyrene-foam seal

Yellow House in Flims

Architect: Valerio Olgiati, Zurich

The yellow house has now been painted white and stands like a built manifesto at the heart of the Swiss ski resort in the Grisons. In the past, it contained a greengrocer's shop and a number of dwellings, but for decades prior to its refurbishment it had stood empty. The architect's father bequeathed his extensive collection of art and cultural artefacts from the area to the community with the proviso that the yellow house should be renovated and converted to exhibit these works. The legacy was also tied to design conditions, which included painting the house white and covering the roof with stone slabs. The concept sought to create an urban focus with cultural amenities at a point of the village centre where a busy through road dissects the community. The entrance has been moved from the road to a newly designed forecourt on one side, where an exposed concrete staircase leans against the building. The gable, the eaves projection and the horizontal elements that once articulated the facade have been removed. The eaves have been raised in height, and the roof is now enclosed by a peripheral concrete tie beam. The rectangular window openings were reduced in size with splayed concrete surrounds that create a slightly conical effect, thereby accentuating the great thickness of the walls (now 80 cm). All these new elements are united with the existing rubble stone walling by the white limewash facade finish. The building was gutted. The windows are now finished flush with the inner face of the walls, but are set off from the smooth internal linings by means of peripheral shadow joints. The new larch soffit beams, supported by wood-stud linings to the inner face of the external walls, are independent of the existing structure. A massive, asymmetrically positioned timber column articulates the exhibition spaces. In the attic storey, it veers diagonally to the tip of the tent-like roof, forming a deliberately irrational feature.

Section
Ground floor plan
First floor plan
scale 1:250

1 Entrance
2 Wheelchair entrance,
  Deliveries
3 Exhibition and
  other events
4 Kitchenette
5 Escape route

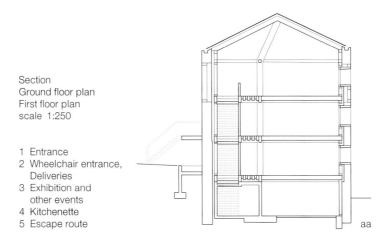

aa

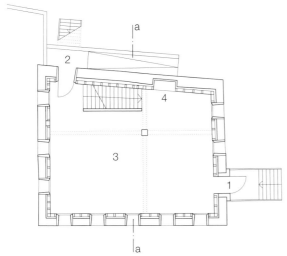

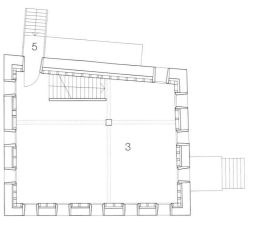

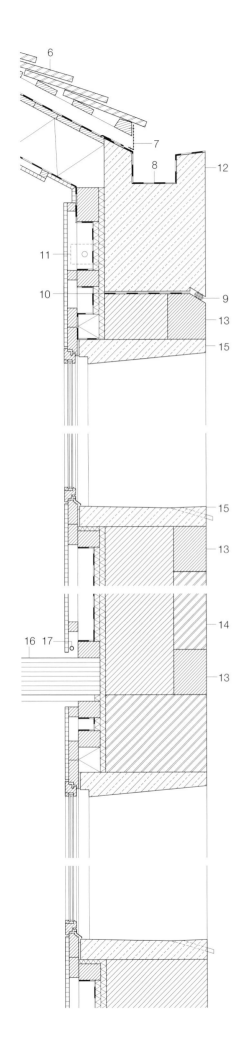

Vertical section through facade
Horizontal section through
entrance
scale 1:20

1 approx. 600 mm existing rubble stone wall
  2× 30 mm thermal insulation
  vapour barrier
  80/120 mm timber studding supporting floor
  60/60 mm battens
  19 mm blockboard
2 in-situ concrete door surround and canopy
3 Ø 80 mm drainpipe
4 glazed oak entrance door, painted
5 doormat
6 roof construction:
  Vals stone slabs, painted white
  120/30 mm battens
  80/80 mm counter-battens
  roof sealing layer
  27 mm wood boarding
  260 mm thermal insulation between
  120/260 mm rafters
  vapour-retarding layer
  19 mm perforated blockboard
7 perforated sheet-metal strip
8 liquid-film seal to gutter
9 butyl-rubber sealing strip
10 bituminous-felt damp-proof course
11 steel fixing lug for timber studding
12 550 mm concrete peripheral tie beam with
   gutter and splayed top edges; limewashed
13 existing horizontal strip
14 existing stone infill panel
   approx. 350 mm brick backing
   2× 30 mm thermal insulation
   vapour barrier
   80/120 mm timber studding supporting floor
   60/60 mm battens
   19 mm blockboard
15 in-situ concrete window surround
   Ø 20 mm PVC drainpipe
16 floor construction: 120/240 mm and
   120/210 mm alternating larch beams
17 heating return pipe

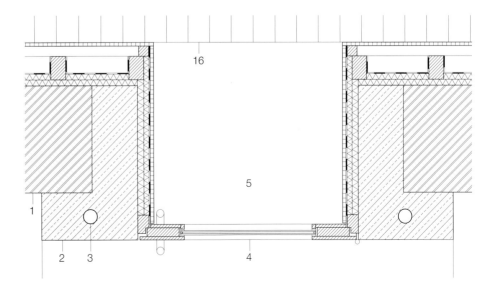

House and Studio Building in Sent

Architects: Rolf Furrer, Basle
Christof Rösch, Sent

Externally, the conversion of this traditional Swiss farmhouse in the Upper Engadine is scarcely visible, although the farm-working areas have been completely redesigned. Based on the principle of a house within a house, an independent three-storey structure has been inserted into the existing building. The new tract, developed by the architect in collaboration with an artist, houses two studios and the bathrooms. It has a mainly timber structure supported on steel columns and concrete slabs and stands clearly set back from the outer walls of the old farmhouse. To facilitate the movement of materials within the building, hatches were formed in the floors of the studios, creating a direct link from the upper storey to the basement, where the artist has his store and a workshop. A movable staircase element connects the entrance level with the sculpting studio at a somewhat lower level.

The sensitive conversion of former agricultural buildings presents a conservational challenge encountered in many rural areas that are subject to structural change. The introverted solution chosen here preserves the outward appearance of the house, while creating the contemplative working atmosphere required by the artist. The window openings in the newly inserted tract, for example, do not afford direct views out. Through them, one sees sections of the old walls of the building framed in a pictorial form. One opening is covered externally by the old ornamental timbers of the former barn facade, while beyond the glazed south wall of the studio, the inner face of the external wall is visible. With its deeply incised rectangular window openings, it resembles a stage set, an effect that is heightened in the evening by the indirect lighting. Only at one point does the autonomous new structure pierce the old facade: a recognizably new studio window and loggia overlook the narrow alleyway behind the house. The new roof lights are visible externally as inconspicuous areas of glazing.

Section · Floor plans
scale 1:400

1 Entrance level
2 Sculpting studio at lower level
3 Studio flat
4 Timber floor of new structure
5 Existing solid floor

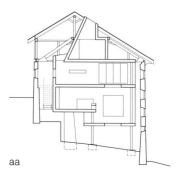

aa

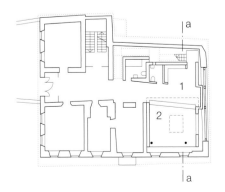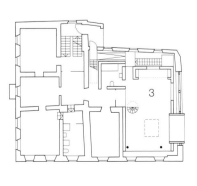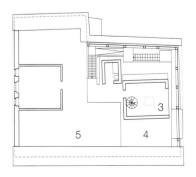

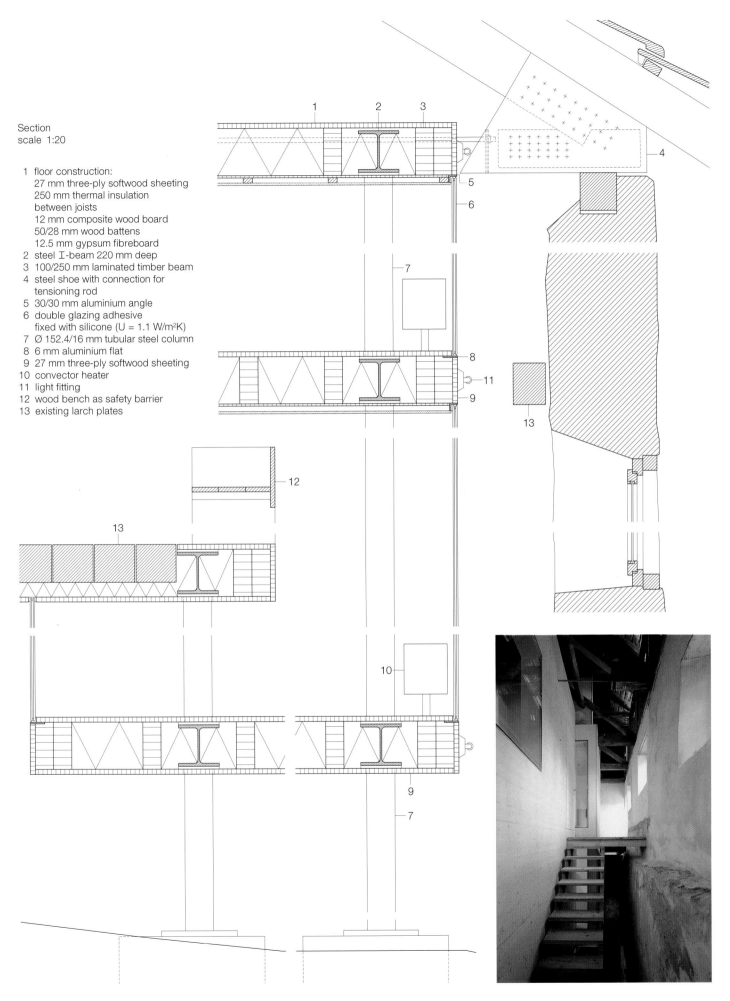

Section
scale 1:20

1 floor construction:
  27 mm three-ply softwood sheeting
  250 mm thermal insulation
  between joists
  12 mm composite wood board
  50/28 mm wood battens
  12.5 mm gypsum fibreboard
2 steel I-beam 220 mm deep
3 100/250 mm laminated timber beam
4 steel shoe with connection for
  tensioning rod
5 30/30 mm aluminium angle
6 double glazing adhesive
  fixed with silicone (U = 1.1 W/m²K)
7 Ø 152.4/16 mm tubular steel column
8 6 mm aluminium flat
9 27 mm three-ply softwood sheeting
10 convector heater
11 light fitting
12 wood bench as safety barrier
13 existing larch plates

Church Community Centre in Schwindkirchen

Architects: arc Architects, Munich

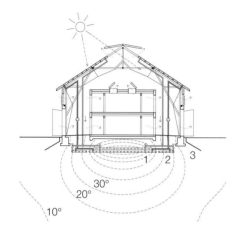

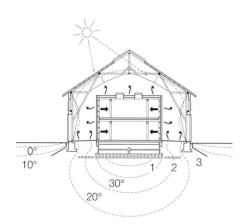

At first sight, the old presbytery in Schwindkirchen seems unchanged. The historical ensemble, consisting of the church, the priest's and curate's houses and a barn (a former grain store), is laid out around a planted courtyard. What lies behind the walls of the old barn is revealed only in summer, when the doors are opened wide and the winter layer of casements is removed, allowing a view into the interior. A new community centre, a reddish-brown timber structure, has been inserted within the existing enclosure of the barn.

The old agricultural building is of no great historical value, but it would not have been possible to demolish it to make room for the new structure. The area required for the community centre was anyway smaller than that of the barn, and to keep the ensemble intact, the architects decided to retain the outer enclosure and to insert a box-like structure inside. In this way, they not only established an attractive spatial dialogue; the solution also allowed the existing facade to be refurbished relatively simply. It was not necessary, for example, to apply elaborate insulation, to install double glazing, or to dry out the old walls completely. Most importantly, though, the concept allowed the retention of the open timber roof structure.

To facilitate an unimpeded use of the internal space, the old columns in the middle of the barn were removed, and the timber trusses are now reinforced with steel rods and plates. The existing load-bearing structure is spanned over the new community centre, and sunlight entering through the ridge lantern creates an interplay of light and shade on the new timber box. Its dark-brown coloration is clearly contrasted with the whitewashed walls of the old barn. The two-storey community centre, containing club and youth rooms and a main hall, consists of prefabricated wall and floor elements in a composite timber-and-concrete form of construction. As part of the energy concept, solar absorbers were installed in the roof of the old barn to provide heating. In winter, solar heat stored in the ground beneath the core structure is yielded as thermal energy via the walls of the community centre to heat the interior and the intermediate spaces. In this way, the damp outer brick walls can gradually be dried out as well.

The attractive interplay between internal and external space becomes fully apparent when the barn gates and the sliding doors of the parish hall are open in summer. The intermediate zone becomes part of the external realm, and the outdoor space flows into the building. The intermediate zone is not just a buffer space, but a covered area available to the community for all kinds of events.

The architects have succeeded in allowing each structure its own identity and nevertheless interlinking them spatially.

Concept for indoor climate
Summer: storage of energy
Winter: release of energy
Sections   scale 1:500
Floor plan   scale 1:500

1 Core storage   3 Insulation
  area   4 Hall
2 Peripheral   5 Club room
  storage area   6 Kitchen

Sectional details
of core structure
scale 1:20

1 roof construction:
   30 mm three-ply laminated sheeting
   160 mm thermal insulation
   22 mm boarding
   12.5 mm gypsum fibreboard
2 floor construction:
   40 mm softwood boarding, bleached and
   white oiled
   50 mm impact-sound insulation between
   wood battens
   100 mm reinforced concrete slab
   30 mm three-ply laminated sheeting with
   water-repellent paint
   12.5 mm gypsum fibreboard
3 wall construction:
   26/120 mm wood boarding
   nail fixed and painted
   black windproof paper
   120 mm thermal insulation between
   60/120 mm timber studs
   22 mm oriented-strand board
   cavity for warming wall/
   services cavity between 60/70 mm
   timber posts
   12.5 mm gypsum fibreboard

Loft Conversion in Berlin

Architects: Rudolf + Sohn, Munich

Erected in 1910 as the rear courtyard section of a typical Berlin block development, this five-storey building served as a cigarette factory and tobacco store until the Second World War. Over the years, changes in its commercial use led to repeated conversions and extensions. The load-bearing structure consists of a riveted steel skeleton frame. The east facade, which is visible from the street, is faced with white engineering bricks. As part of the rehabilitation programme for the building, bricks of the same kind were specially manufactured to replace those that were damaged or missing. The other facades are rendered. In renewing the attic storey and inserting a gallery level, the architects had to observe the existing eaves and ridge heights. As part of the refurbishment, the former timber rafters were replaced with steel members, and the existing structural framed girders have been left exposed. The provision of two escape staircases meant that it was possible to do without a fire-resisting coating to the roof structure. While the entire lower section of the mansard now consists of a glazed post-and-rail construction with horizontal aluminium glazing strips, the upper roof slopes are covered with titanium-zinc sheeting. In the middle of the attic storey is a discussion space enclosed in butt-jointed frameless glazing, with access via black, wood sliding doors. The colour of the shelving, which consists of clear-varnished wood fibreboard, forms a contrast to the otherwise black, white and grey aesthetic. Newly introduced materials such as the asphalt flooring or the steel sections, gratings and light fittings, which are galvanized or painted with micaceous iron oxide, reflect the industrial context of the building.

Section • Floor plan   scale 1:500

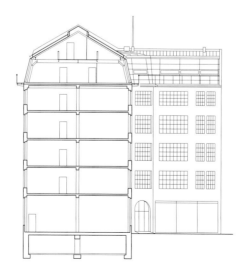
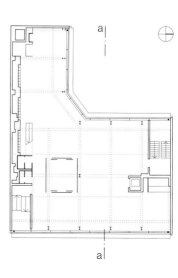

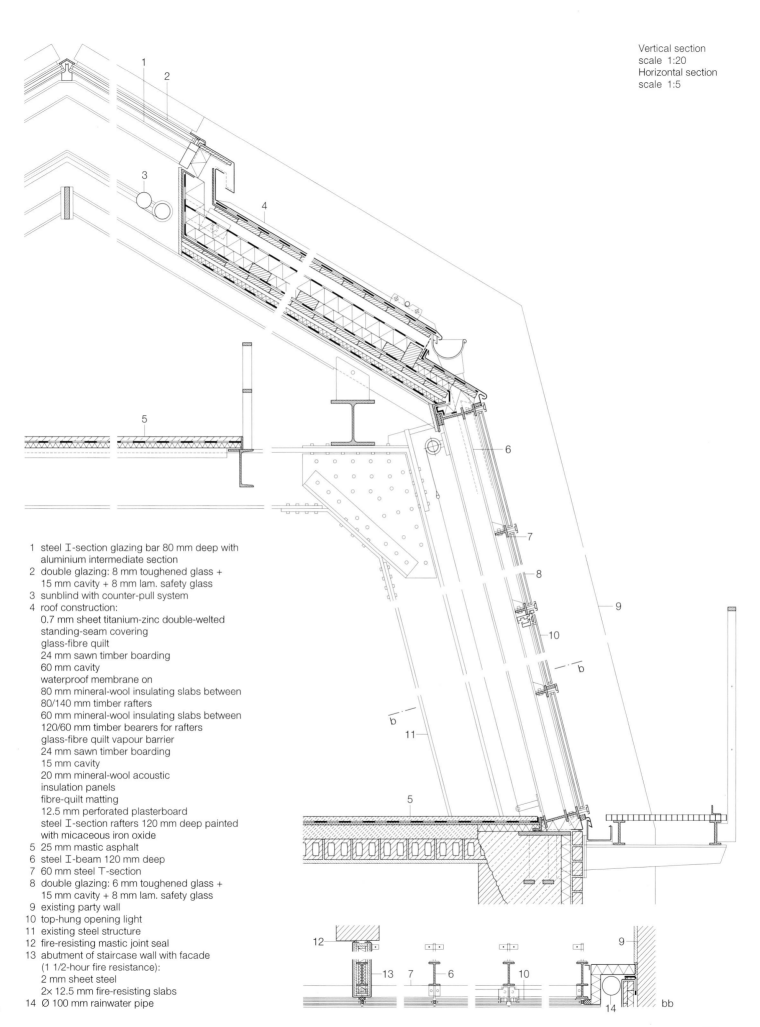

Vertical section
scale 1:20
Horizontal section
scale 1:5

1 steel I-section glazing bar 80 mm deep with
  aluminium intermediate section
2 double glazing: 8 mm toughened glass +
  15 mm cavity + 8 mm lam. safety glass
3 sunblind with counter-pull system
4 roof construction:
  0.7 mm sheet titanium-zinc double-welted
  standing-seam covering
  glass-fibre quilt
  24 mm sawn timber boarding
  60 mm cavity
  waterproof membrane on
  80 mm mineral-wool insulating slabs between
  80/140 mm timber rafters
  60 mm mineral-wool insulating slabs between
  120/60 mm timber bearers for rafters
  glass-fibre quilt vapour barrier
  24 mm sawn timber boarding
  15 mm cavity
  20 mm mineral-wool acoustic
  insulation panels
  fibre-quilt matting
  12.5 mm perforated plasterboard
  steel I-section rafters 120 mm deep painted
  with micaceous iron oxide
5 25 mm mastic asphalt
6 steel I-beam 120 mm deep
7 60 mm steel T-section
8 double glazing: 6 mm toughened glass +
  15 mm cavity + 8 mm lam. safety glass
9 existing party wall
10 top-hung opening light
11 existing steel structure
12 fire-resisting mastic joint seal
13 abutment of staircase wall with facade
  (1 1/2-hour fire resistance):
  2 mm sheet steel
  2× 12.5 mm fire-resisting slabs
14 Ø 100 mm rainwater pipe

79

House Extension in Montrouge

Architects: Fabienne Couvert & Guillaume Terver, Paris
IN SITU montréal, Montreal

The site, with its stock of walnut and lemon trees, belongs to a landscape artist and is located in a suburb of Paris. The garden is screened from the road by the existing limestone house, which dates from the beginning of the 20th century. The two cubic extension structures in timber face on to the sheltered garden. In the layout of the rooms, a distinction was made between private spaces, semi-private spaces, and those areas accessible to visitors. The entrance, situated at the junction between the new and existing sections of the house, leads directly into the living room, which in turn opens on to the garden via a large showcase window. Immediately adjoining this space are the artist's studio, and the dining room in the existing building. Above the studio is a sleeping gallery. The children's rooms are situated on the upper floor and in the attic storey of the existing house. All materials in the older part of the building were retained, including the parquet flooring, tiling, stucco work, the wood stairs and the cast-iron radiators. To emphasize the additive nature of the extension, the two new volumes were designed in different ways: one with a smooth, varnished wood facade with invisible joints, the other with joints accentuated by cover strips. What the two volumes have in common is their timber-frame construction and the dark polished surfaces of the walls and fittings. Exotic woods were used internally and externally, ensuring a sense of continuity and unity in the design, and creating a series of flowing spatial transitions. The large, gate-like pivoting shutters, with which the glazed openings on the ground floor can be closed, are like variable furnishings. In an open position, they form an extension of the external side walls, with which they sit flush. This theme is continued internally by the pivoting wood panels that are used to darken the sleeping gallery above the studio. Here, shelf-like elements function as a supporting structure, balustrade and desktop.

Section • Floor plans
scale 1:250

1 Dining room
2 Living room
3 Studio
4 Sleeping gallery
5 Children's room
6 Guest room

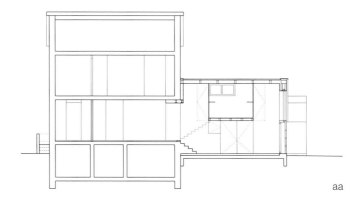

aa

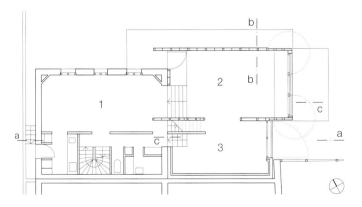

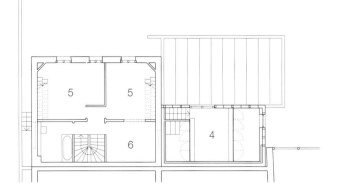

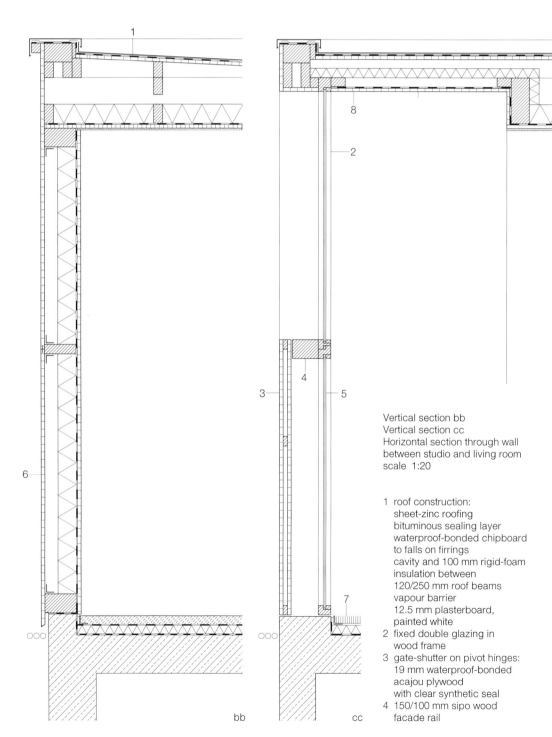

Vertical section bb
Vertical section cc
Horizontal section through wall
between studio and living room
scale 1:20

1 roof construction:
   sheet-zinc roofing
   bituminous sealing layer
   waterproof-bonded chipboard
   to falls on firrings
   cavity and 100 mm rigid-foam
   insulation between
   120/250 mm roof beams
   vapour barrier
   12.5 mm plasterboard,
   painted white
2 fixed double glazing in
   wood frame
3 gate-shutter on pivot hinges:
   19 mm waterproof-bonded
   acajou plywood
   with clear synthetic seal
4 150/100 mm sipo wood
   facade rail

5 casement door with double
   glazing
6 wall construction:
   19 mm waterproof-bonded
   acajou plywood
   with clear synthetic seal
   cavity and rigid-foam
   insulation between
   150/120 mm wood framing
   vapour barrier
   19 mm MDF,
   smoothed and painted
7 door mat
8 sipo wood laminated sheeting
9 wall without rear ventilated
   cavity
10 recess for flush-fitting shutter
11 water-repellent concrete
   threshold

bb   cc

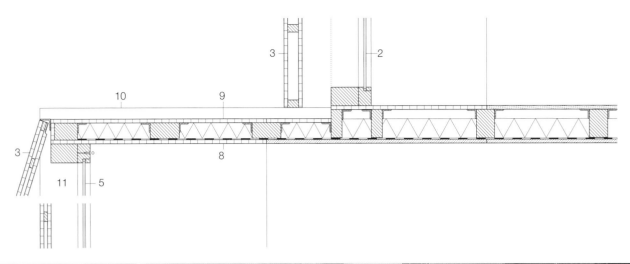

House Extension in Munich

Architects: Lydia Haack + John Höpfner, Munich

The client wished to extend this small 1950s house, which forms part of an estate development idyllically set on a lake. Additional space for a dining room and study were created over the existing garage, with access to a terrace covered by a pergola. The extension is brightly lit and has a general quality of lightness. The terrace forms an ideal, sunlit sitting area and viewing point, protected from the wind and the noise from the nearby autobahn on the garden side to the west.

The load-bearing structure of the extension consists of laminated timber posts and beams connected to each other with flat crossed stainless-steel brackets. The structure is supported by the existing house and is also braced by the 10 mm MDF slabs – laid out with peripheral shadow joints – that form the internal wall lining. The structural grid is coordinated with the wall and window openings of the house. In this way, a complementary unity is created between the old and new sections of the building, a unity that is reinforced by the links between the internal spaces. The abutment with the existing building is structurally minimalized, yet visually accentuated, by the use of frameless glazing, which continues in the roof light. The outer walls of the extension were executed to a high standard of thermal insulation and are largely airtight.

Shelving units, with an overhead strip of glazing, form a spatial division between the new and existing sections of the house. Container elements and wall slabs inserted between the columns define the individual spatial zones without separating them completely. The extension allowed the creation of a spacious, continuous living area on the ground floor.

Sections
Ground floor plan
scale 1:250

1 Hall
2 Study
3 Dining room
4 Terrace
5 Kitchen
6 Living room

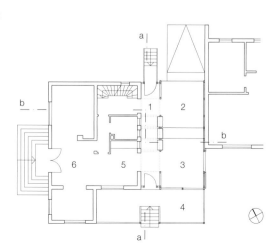

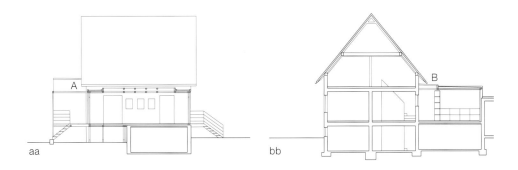

aa   bb

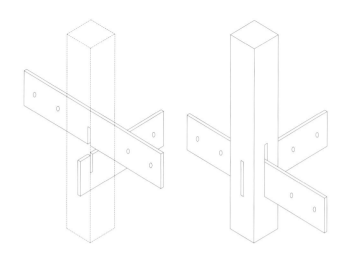

A

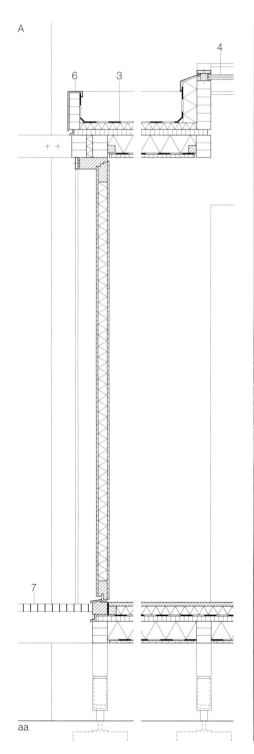

6   3   4

7

aa

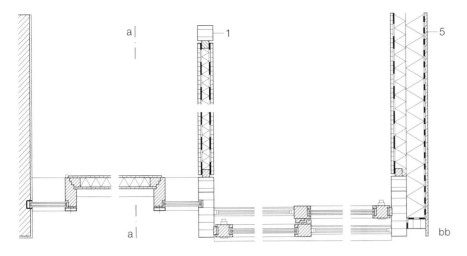

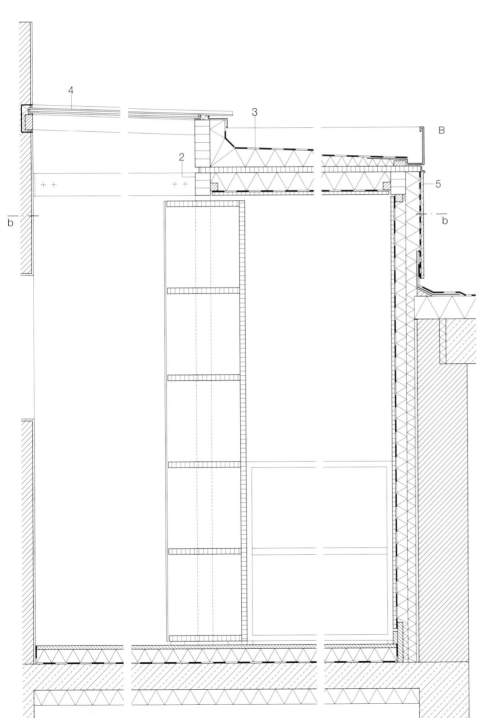

Horizontal section
Vertical sections
scale 1:20

Detail of connection between beam and post
Horizontal section
scale 1:5

1 76/76 mm laminated timber post
2 76/200 mm laminated timber beam
3 roof construction:
    protective matting
    waterproof membrane
    insulation finished to falls (min. 30 mm)
    30 mm laminated wood board
    100 mm thermal insulation
    non-diffusing vapour barrier
    10 mm MDF soffit lining with 10 mm peripheral
    shadow joint
4 double glazing: 6 mm toughened glass +
    12 mm cavity + 8 mm laminated safety glass
5 wall construction:
    10 mm fibre-cement sheeting, painted white
    moisture-diffusing windproof layer
    140 mm thermal insulation
    non-diffusing vapour barrier
    10 mm MDF lining
6 sheet titanium-zinc covering
7 galvanized steel grating to terrace

House on Lake Starnberg

Architects: Fink + Jocher, Munich

Building development on the eastern side of Lake Starnberg consists largely of converted farmhouses, and villas that avail themselves of the easy access to nearby Munich. The present structure is an old farm and fisherman's house, the working sections of which had become so dilapidated that it was not feasible to convert them into living space. As part of the refurbishment, therefore, the front section of the building was demolished and newly erected. The architects were confronted with the task of designing a strictly modern extension, yet in exactly the same form as the previous structure, and using the same materials and coloration. They replaced the small, white-framed windows and green pivoting shutters with large sliding casements and sliding shutters, both of which, when fully open, disappear into the wall construction. Depending on the position of these elements, the facade either has a continuous planar appearance or is articulated by the openings. The quality of these openings becomes evident on the upper floor, where the view of the lake – which seems to come right up to the house – is staged to great effect. The roof, which externally has the appearance of a thin, light slab laid over the building, unites the plain, unornamented extension with the existing structure. Used hitherto as a summer residence, the house now provides a weekend abode for various families. The spatial divisions are flexible. The ground floor contains a bathroom and three small rooms that can be divided off or joined together by means of sliding partitions. On the upper floor, there are two large spaces that can be converted into single-room flats if required and that afford fine views of the lake. These spaces are drawn round the staircase, from which they are divided in part by an area of glazing that allows daylight to enter the hall space. The fumed-oak flooring matches the dark, partly antique furnishings in the old farmhouse and is contrasted with the white walls.

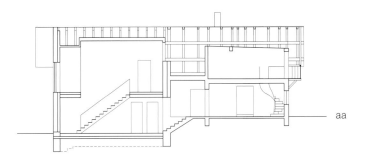

aa

Longitudinal section
Ground floor plan
First floor plan
scale 1:250

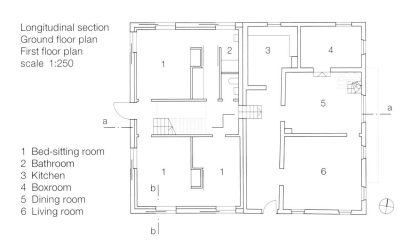

1 Bed-sitting room
2 Bathroom
3 Kitchen
4 Boxroom
5 Dining room
6 Living room

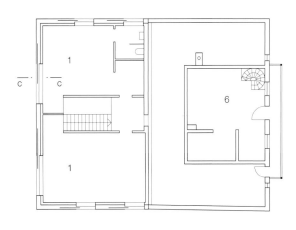

Vertical section through facade
scale 1:20

1 polymer-bitumen shingles
   bituminous roof sealing membrane
   24 mm tongued-and-grooved boarding
   180 mm mineral-wool thermal insulation between
   80/180 mm rafters
   30 mm mineral-wool thermal insulation between
   50/30 mm battens
   vapour barrier
   50/30 mm counter-battens
   12.5 mm plasterboard
2 120/100 mm timber purlin
3 42 mm three-ply laminated sheeting
   with brown glazed finish
4 120/100 mm eaves timber
5 27 mm wrot softwood boarding
   with brown glazed finish
   100/120 mm studding and counter-studding
   windproof building paper
   15 mm oriented-strand board
   120 mm mineral-wool thermal insulation between
   60/120 mm timber studding
   vapour barrier
   15 mm oriented-strand board
   60/40 mm battens/40 mm services cavity
   2× 12.5 mm plasterboard
6 sliding shutter softwood
   with brown glazed finish
7 wood sliding window with double glazing
8 rainwater channel,
   adhesive fixed with silicone
9 water spout
10 insect screen
11 22 mm fumed-oak parquet
   65 mm screed around underfloor heating
   separating layer
   20 mm polystyrene impact-sound insulation
   25 mm oriented-strand board
   120 mm mineral-wool
   thermal insulation between
   140/200 mm timber joists
   27 mm spring strip
   12.5 mm plasterboard
12 22 mm fumed-oak parquet
   65 mm screed around underfloor heating
   separating layer
   20 mm polystyrene impact-sound insulation
   80 mm polystyrene thermal insulation
   sealing layer
   160 mm reinforced concrete floor slab
   50 mm blinding
   200 mm bed of gravel

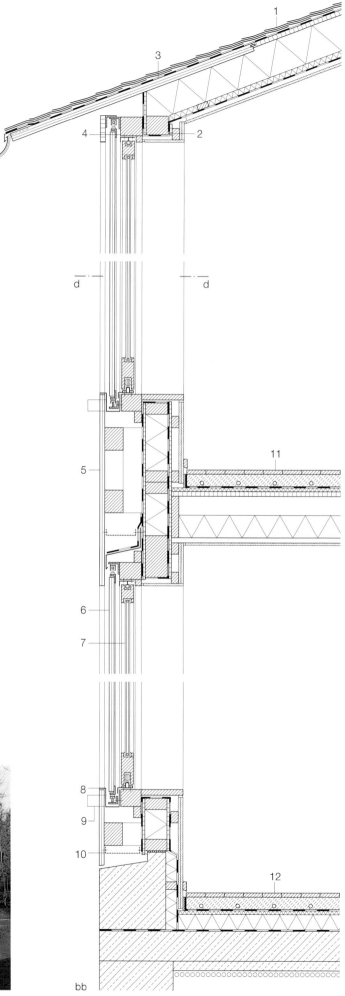

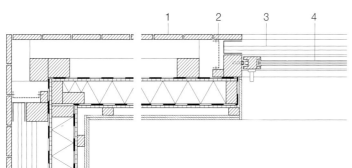
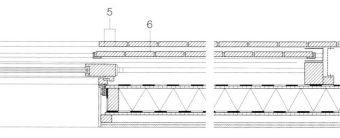

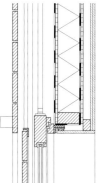

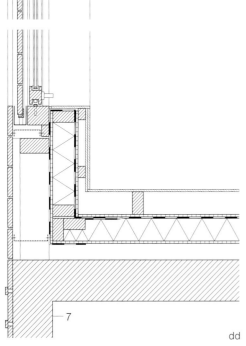

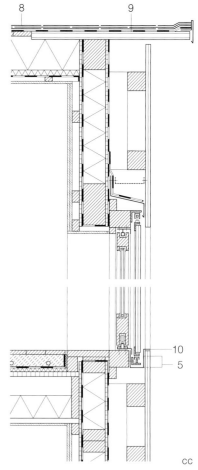

Horizontal section through facade
Vertical section through verge of roof
scale 1:20

1 27 mm wrot softwood boarding
  with brown glazed finish
  100/120 mm studding and
  counter-studding
  windproof building paper
  15 mm oriented-strand board
  120 mm mineral-wool thermal
  insulation between
  60/120 mm timber studding
  vapour barrier
  15 mm oriented-strand board
  60/40 mm battens/40 mm services
  cavity
  2× 12.5 mm plasterboard
2 insect screen
3 shutter track on 60/40/5 mm angle
4 wood sliding window with double
  glazing
5 water spout
6 sliding shutter: 27 mm softwood
  boarding with brown glazed finish
  in 45/30/5 mm angle frame
7 existing structure
8 polymer-bitumen shingles
  bituminous roof sealing membrane
  24 mm tongued-and-grooved
  boarding
  180 mm mineral-wool thermal
  insulation between
  80/180 mm timber rafters
  30 mm mineral-wool thermal
  insulation between
  50/30 mm battens
  vapour barrier
  50/30 mm counter-battens
  12.5 mm plasterboard
9 42 mm three-ply laminated
  sheeting
10 rainwater channel, adhesive fixed
   with silicone

dd

cc

House Extension in Remscheid

Architects: Gerhard Kalhöfer, Stefan Korschildgen, Cologne

In front of the existing small house is a large, intensively culti-vated garden. The clients, who live on the ground floor, wished to extend the habitable area and create a closer link with the outdoor realm, which was previously accessible only via an internal basement staircase. A flexible structure was created, the special nature of which is underlined by the choice of materials. The form of the new tract corresponds exactly with that of an earlier extension dating from the 1950s.

The new volume is raised on a supporting structure, consisting of steel square hollow sections. Heavy-duty industrial rollers in channel-section tracks allow the entire extension to be moved backwards and forwards. During the warmer months of the year, it can be slid aside, opening up a platform at ground floor level which can be used as a terrace. The platform consists of metal gratings that allow light to penetrate to the area beneath. The balustrade can be simply dismantled when the structure is slid back into its original position. A narrow staircase between the old and new extensions provides access from the ground floor of the main building to the garden. The staircase space between the two structures remains open even when the new extension is moved back to its "winter position".

The outer skin of the new tract consists of transparent, rigid corrugated PVC sheeting with a ventilated cavity to the rear. The internal skin comprises an insulated timber-frame construc-tion lined on both faces with plywood. To prevent overheating of the internal space, the outer layer of plywood is covered with a nylon-reinforced reflective fabric. The electrical installation is visible in the cavity behind the transparent corrugated sheeting. If the need arises, the simple wood-frame construction can be easily removed, allowing the building to be converted without difficulty to other uses – for example, into a greenhouse.

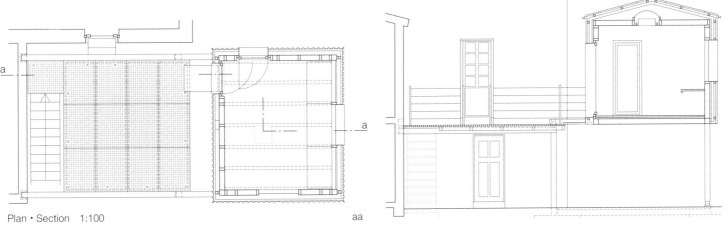

Plan · Section 1:100

aa

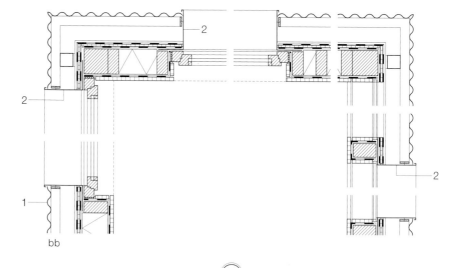

bb

Floor plan · Section   scale 1:20

1 wall construction:
  rigid corrugated PVC sheeting 76/18 mm
  50/50/4 mm galvanized steel SHS rails
  70/70/4 mm galvanized steel SHS posts
  1 mm reflective fabric
  10 mm plywood sheeting with glazed finish
  0.8 mm water-repellent windproof layer
  140 mm insulated wood-framed structure
  0.2 mm polythene sheet vapour barrier
  19 mm plywood sheeting with glazed finish
2 0.8 mm sheet-zinc surround
3 clear perspex domed roof light
4 matt perspex surround
5 fluorescent lighting strip
6 roof-light lock
7 bituminous roof sealing layer, sanded and
  with reflective coating
8 40 mm reconstructed stone slabs on
  foamed sheet underlayer
9 4 mm aluminium chequerplate bridge with
  upturned edges
10 30 mm metal grating
11 150/150 mm steel SHS supporting frame
12 heavy-duty roller in channel-section track
  fixed on 150/150/7.1 mm steel SHSs
13 Ø 38 mm galvanized steel tubular balustrade
  post and nylon cables

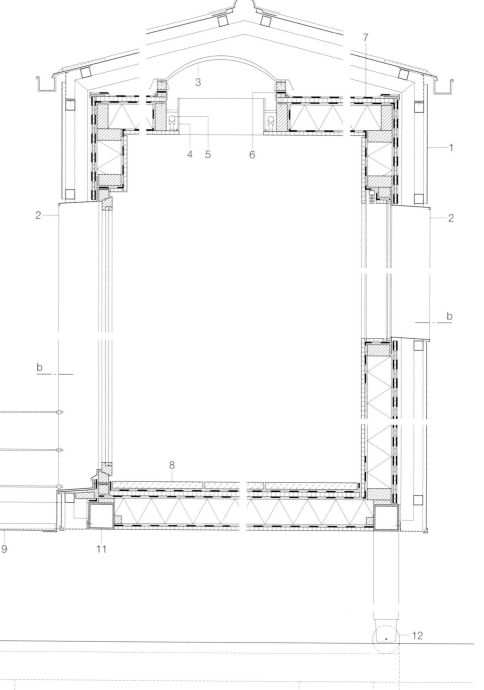

Parasite in Rotterdam

Architects: Korteknie & Stuhlmacher, Rotterdam

A special object now occupies the roof of a lift shaft in the former Las Palmas workshop building in Rotterdam harbour. The apple-green structure is the first of a series of similar objects to be realized as part of a Dutch architectural project bearing the name "Parasites". Despite its small size, it is visible from afar. The scheme is an appeal to treat urban space in an innovative way.

"Parasites" are lightweight, movable, low-cost structures that are placed in unusual or seemingly impossible urban situations and exploit the existing infrastructure. This prototype was designed to strike a new note on the host building. It was to have an economical form of construction, be capable of reuse elsewhere and be eco-friendly. Other aspects that had to be considered were the specific constraints of the rooftop location, including the load-bearing capacity of the supporting structure, in conjunction with high wind loading and crane costs. The requirements were met with a low-weight laminated glued timber structure, which permitted a high degree of pre-fabrication and great latitude in the design of the overall form and the layout of open and closed surfaces.

The impregnated laminated boarding, varnished and colour-coated in part, was manufactured in various thicknesses to meet structural needs and to provide the required level of insulation. Within four days, the elements were erected on a previously assembled steel supporting structure. The parasite was then connected to the water and power supplies of the workshop building by means of flexible couplings, and finally completed with internal finishings and frameless glazing. The windows lend this display dwelling a sense of spaciousness that is in striking contrast to the dark access staircase in the host building. Some of the windows offer panoramic views across the harbour; others are smaller and focus on specific aspects of the surroundings.

The Las Palmas structure, used by the city of Rotterdam as part of its "cultural capital" programme in 2001, is still a venue for various activities, including the architectural biennale. Since the conclusion of the cultural events of 2001, the parasite has been used as a discussion, exhibition and office space. For the time being, it may stay where it is – as long as the future of the host building remains undecided.

Plan · Section
scale 1:400

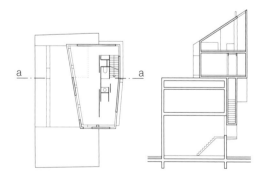

a · · · · · · · · · · · a

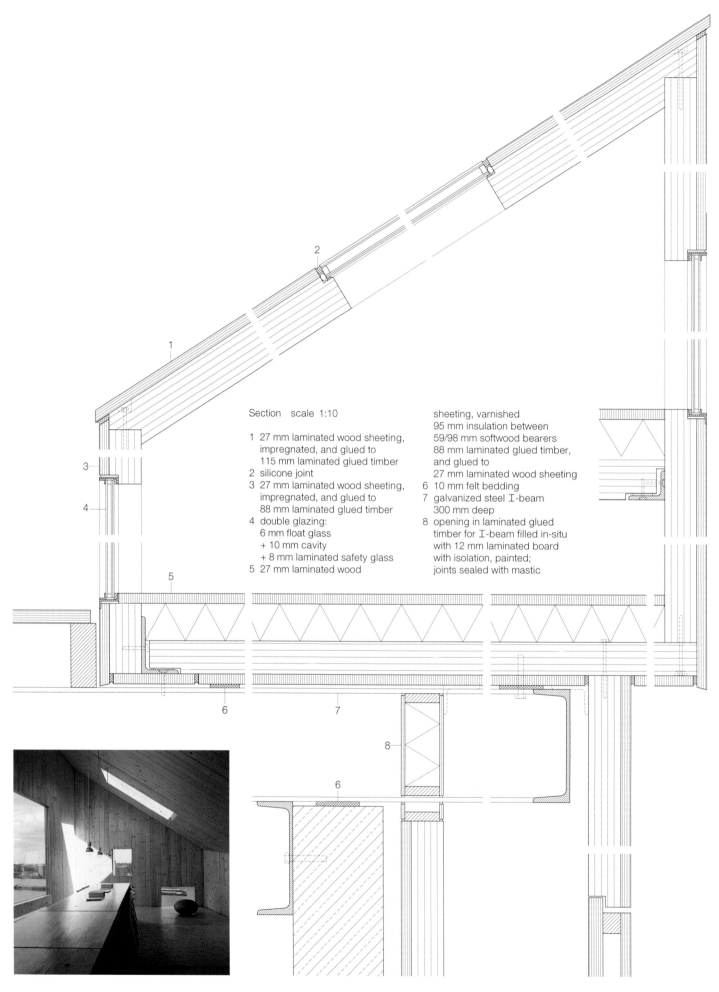

Section scale 1:10

1 27 mm laminated wood sheeting,
   impregnated, and glued to
   115 mm laminated glued timber
2 silicone joint
3 27 mm laminated wood sheeting,
   impregnated, and glued to
   88 mm laminated glued timber
4 double glazing:
   6 mm float glass
   + 10 mm cavity
   + 8 mm laminated safety glass
5 27 mm laminated wood

sheeting, varnished
95 mm insulation between
59/98 mm softwood bearers
88 mm laminated glued timber,
and glued to
27 mm laminated wood sheeting
6 10 mm felt bedding
7 galvanized steel I-beam
   300 mm deep
8 opening in laminated glued
   timber for I-beam filled in-situ
   with 12 mm laminated board
   with isolation, painted;
   joints sealed with mastic

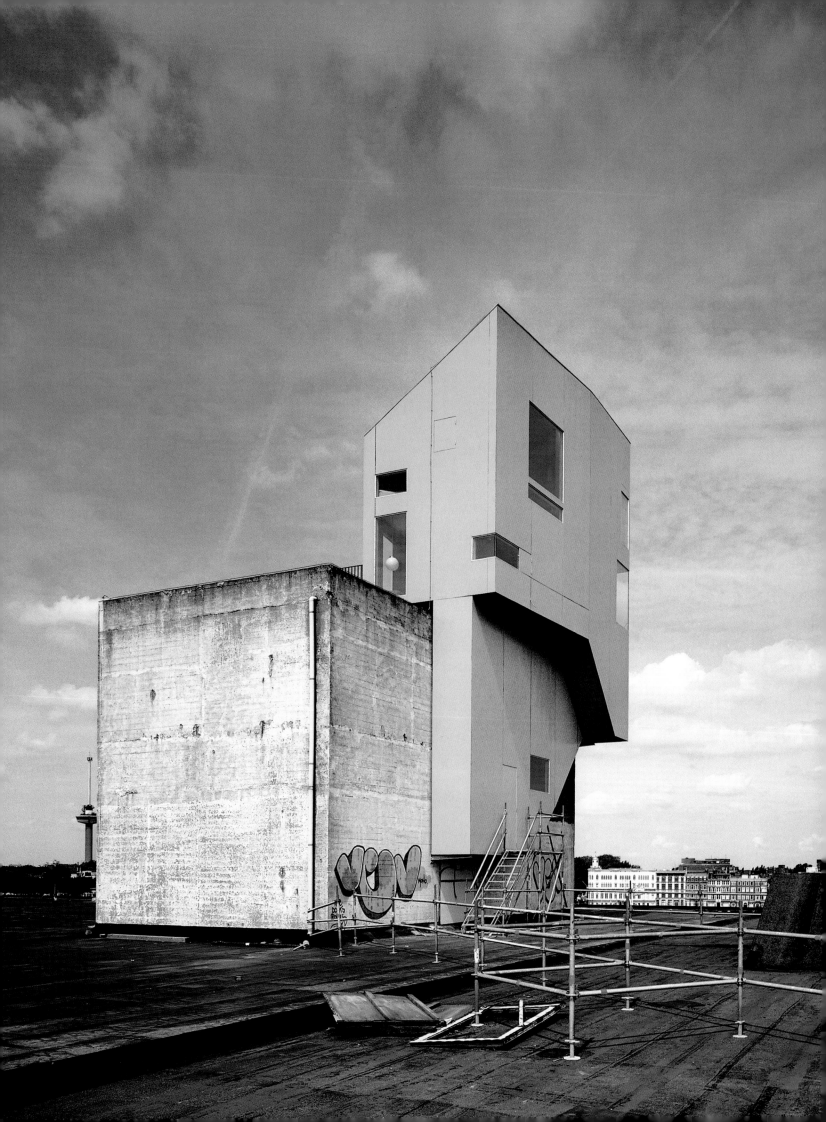

Restaurant in Oporto

Architects: Guilherme Páris Couto, Oporto

The River Douro rises in the mountains of northern Spain and winds its way for nearly 900 kilometres, at first through bare rocky valleys and in its lower course through a fertile terraced landscape with vineyards and olive groves, until it finally flows into the Atlantic near the Portuguese city of Oporto. Here, a long-term urban planning project has been implemented to activate the riverside space and to upgrade the road strip that leads along the Douro to the old city centre. As part of these measures, a disused cargo boat has been transformed with simple means into a restaurant. The boat is held in position by two steel masts driven into the river bed and left in a untreated state.

A sloping gangway leads down from the river bank to the pontoon-like structure of the former ship. Passing between high walls that screen the restaurant from the bustle of the shore, visitors are surprised by the broad view of the river that suddenly unfolds before them. The other three sides of the restaurant are fully glazed with large opening elements that create a flowing transition between internal and external space. A steel platform with a wood-plank deck has been constructed on the old vessel, and set on top of this is the small cubic structure in steel and glass that houses the dining room. In warm weather, it can be extended on to the terrace-like deck. The roof, supported by the wall slabs and a single steel column, seems to cantilever out freely over its full width. Many of the details are reminiscent of marine architecture, and a combination of materials was used in fitting out the ship: sheet copper, steel and glass, fibre-cement sheeting and dark kambala wood. Separate flights of stairs link the terrace with the kitchen and the toilet area, both of which are housed in the former hold below deck.

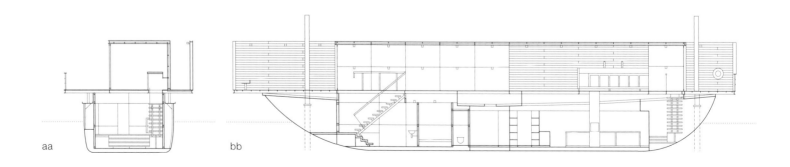

aa   bb

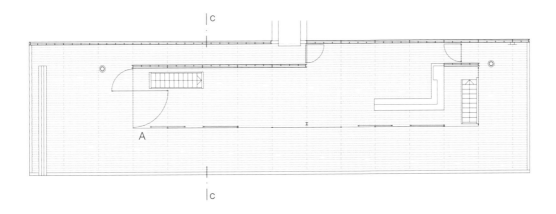

Sections
Floor plans
scale 1:200

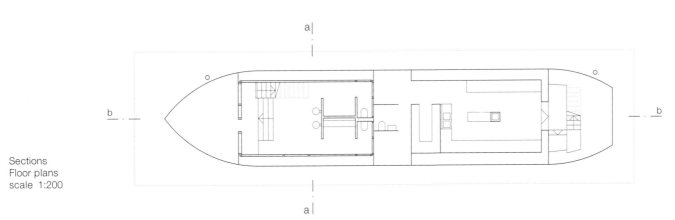

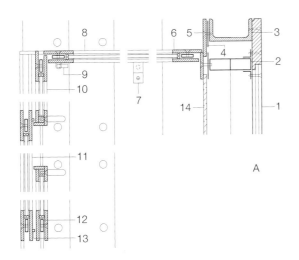

A

Horizontal section through
corner of restaurant
Vertical section
scale 1:10

1 25 mm kambala wood planks
2 60/30 mm steel RHS
3 120 mm steel channel
4 70/5 mm steel flat
5 100/8 mm steel flat
6 80/8 mm steel flat
7 stainless-steel pivot
8 pivoting door
9 locking bolt
10 sliding door
11 fixed glazing

12 40/15 mm steel RHS
13 8/8 mm steel bar
14 8 mm fibre-cement sheeting
15 fabric covering
16 160 mm steel channel
17 50/50/6 mm steel angle
18 30/30/5 mm steel angle
19 40 mm kambala wood planks
20 10 mm fibre-cement sheeting
21 60/60 mm timber studs
22 0.8 mm sheet-copper roofing

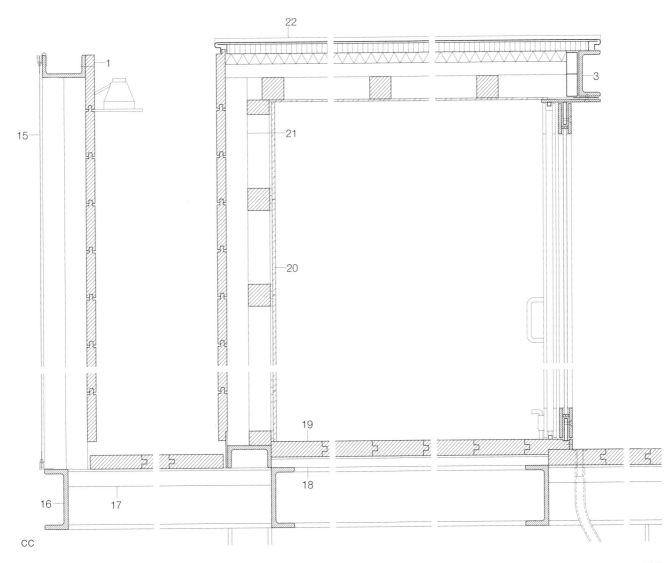

CC

Panel Construction Housing in Dresden

Architects: Knerer and Lang, Dresden

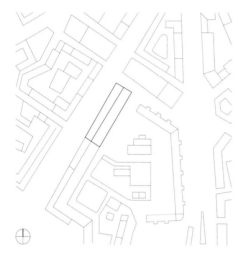

In the new inner city, opposite the historical centre of Dresden, part of the surviving Baroque urban fabric was replaced by new concrete slab developments (type WBS 70) in the post-war period. The housing blocks were erected along the historical street building lines, using construction elements specially developed for this purpose. These included precast concrete balcony parapet walls, the surfaces of which were finished with a reddish-brown ceramic mosaic. On the ground floor, an extensive strip of shops was installed to enliven the newly created pedestrian zone.
In the meantime, the balcony balustrades had become seriously dilapidated, and the client – a municipal housing association in Dresden – decided on a comprehensive refurbishment of the facade, with the creation of outdoor sitting areas and non-insulated conservatories. After the removal of the loggia construction, a new steel structure was erected in front of the facade. In response to structural constraints, the extension was designed like a system of shelving fixed to and supported by the existing building. For cost reasons, the architects worked with identical prefabricated elements as far as possible. The balcony floors consist of load-bearing girder grids with a structural depth of 30 cm. The vertical conservatory members are not welded to the rest of the structure. Optimum ventilation of the loggias was achieved through the use of large areas of louvred glazing. In a splayed position, the louvres reflect much of the solar radiation away from the building, so that it was possible to do without sunshading. At the sides, the glazed surrounds are closed by conventional all-glass doors. Wood gratings over the sandwich slabs to the floors form an attractive contrast to the steel-and-glass construction.

Site plan
scale 1:5000

Layout plan: type WBS 70
after facade refurbishment
scale 1:200

1 Living room
2 Kitchen
3 Bedroom
4 Child's room
5 Bathroom/WC
6 Conservatory
7 Balcony

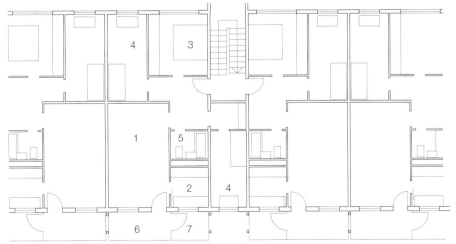

Plan · Section · Elevation
Conservatory and balcony
scale 1:50

Horizontal section
Vertical section
Details
scale 1:10

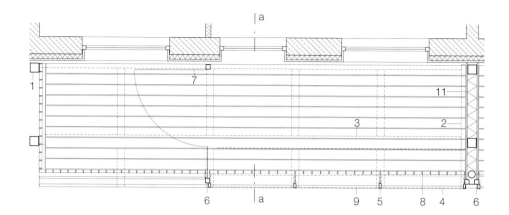

1 120/120/4 mm steel SHS column
2 180 mm steel channel
3 steel I-beam 180 mm deep
4 120 mm steel channel
5 60/30 mm steel RHS facade post
6 50/50/4 mm steel SHS with door hinges or
   glass fixing strip welded on
7 all-glass door
8 50/10 mm steel flat balustrade
9 glass louvres, with etched finish in
   balustrade area
10 floor construction:
   100/30 mm wood strips on
   46/26 mm wood bearers
   sealing layer
   44 mm insulated sandwich panel with
   aluminium sheeting on both faces
11 partition:
   12 mm fibre-cement sheeting
   120 mm insulation
   12 mm fibre-cement sheeting
12 steel I-beam 120 mm deep

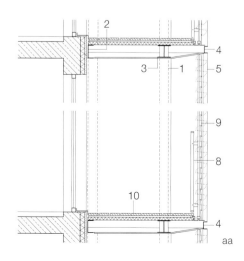

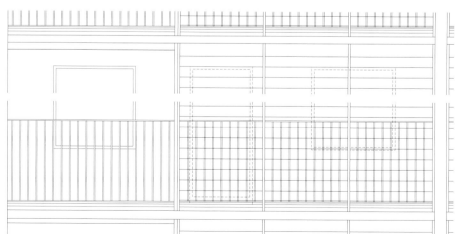

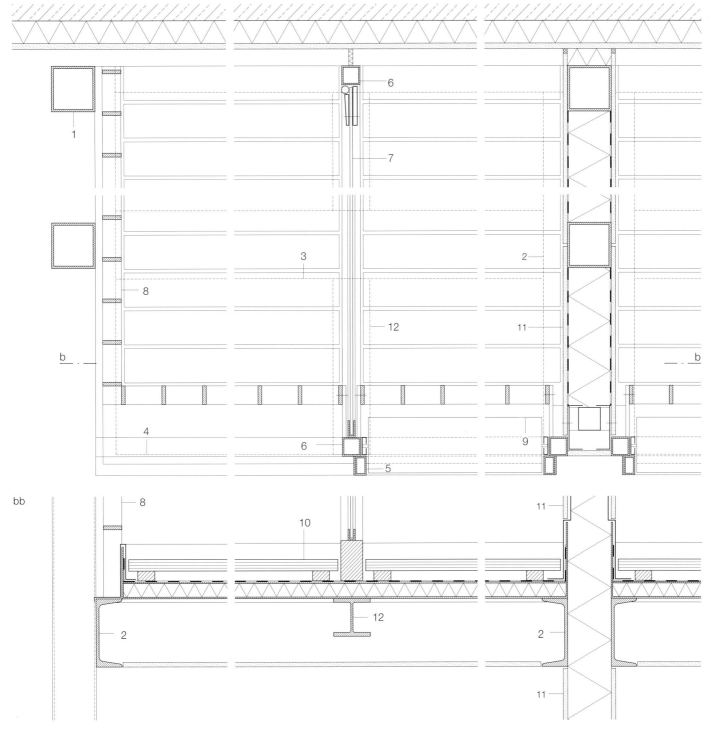

Housing Development in Chur

Architects: Dieter Jüngling and Andreas Hagmann, Chur

Designed in 1942, the Tivoli housing development in Bahn-hofsplatz, Chur, Switzerland, is an unspectacular ensemble of buildings. It was nevertheless deemed worthy of preservation in view of the lack of any clear spatial definition in the surroundings. The seven blocks of flats, articulated into units with two and three dwellings per floor, are laid out along the lines of the roads to create a traditional street-block development. The small flats no longer complied with modern requirements, however, and it was difficult to find new tenants. The restructuring measures included modifying the layouts to meet today's needs and modernizing the staircases, which no longer complied with building regulations. In view of the central location of this estate, it seemed sensible to incorporate additional commercial uses and offices, and to create a higher user density on the site area. The three existing buildings were carefully restored, and additional structures were inserted in the spaces between them. The new sections, set back from the road, tie the estate together to form a continuous ensemble. By relocating the staircases outside the blocks, additional dwelling space was created. Within the closed street block is a landscaped courtyard, where the estate reveals an entirely new aspect. Here, a new layer has been added to the dwellings in the form of a loggia-type strip in front of the original facade. The continuous, fully glazed verandas not only extend the existing dwellings and enhance the habitable quality; they allowed an external layer of insulation to be applied to the old facades, and they create a new buffer zone that greatly improves the energy balance of the compact building volumes. As a result, the existing fabric has been visibly upgraded.

Site plan   scale 1:2000
A Existing development
B New development

Floor plan prior to conversion
Floor plans after conversion
scale 1:500

1 Living room
2 Room
3 Kitchen
4 Office
5 Loggia
6 Bank

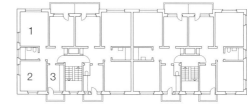

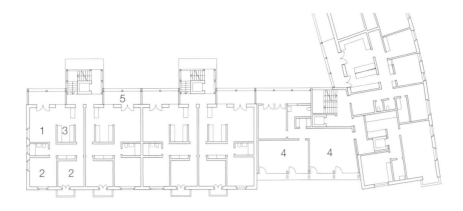

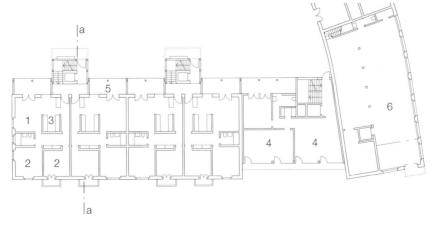

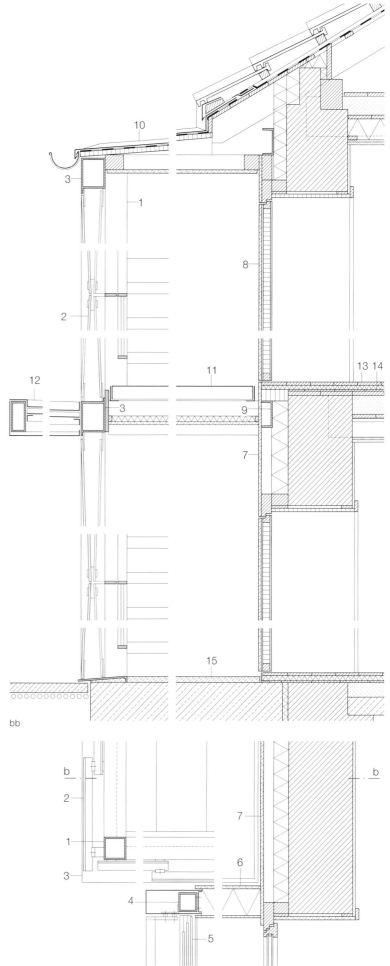

3

1

2

12   3

10

8

11   9

13 14

7

15

bb

b   b

2

1

3

4

5

7

6

Staircase tower on courtyard face
Loggia extension on courtyard face

Vertical sections
Horizontal sections
scale 1:20

1 120/120 mm steel SHS
2 10 mm toughened glass with
   115/50/5 mm steel point fixings
3 120/160 mm steel RHS
4 100/100 mm steel SHS
   2 mm sheet-aluminium cladding
5 10 mm toughened glass sliding element in
   aluminium track
6 16 mm cement-bonded chipboard
   140 mm thermal insulation
   12 mm laminated construction board
7 16 mm cement-bonded chipboard
   60/120 mm steel RHS
   80 mm thermal insulation
   350–410 mm existing brickwork
   15 mm plaster
8 door with 16 mm cement-bonded
   chipboard lining
9 140/60 mm steel channel
10 sheet-copper standing-seam roofing
   separating layer
   27 mm three-ply laminated sheeting
   100/80 mm timber bearers
   16 mm cement-bonded chipboard
11 5–7 mm metal sheeting with
   textured surface, bent to shape
   100/50 mm steel angle frame
   180/100 mm steel RHS
   30 mm cavity insulation
   16 mm cement-bonded chipboard
12 2 mm sheet-steel covering with
   liquid-plastic coating
   30 mm ribbed metal sheeting
   30/30 mm steel angle frame
   160/80 mm steel RHS
13 13 mm oak parquet flooring
   2 mm matting on 16 mm impact-sound
   insulation slab
14 existing floor construction:
   9 mm beech parquet
   21 mm fir boarding
   100 mm loose filling between
   120/220 mm timber joists
   21 mm fir sound boarding
   24 mm gypsum board; 28 mm gypsum plaster
15 30 mm granolithic paving
   250 mm reinforced concrete slab
16 folding shutter: 32/48 mm fir frame with
   12 mm phenolic-resin-coated plywood panel
17 65 mm fir casement with double glazing
18 balustrade: 50/15 mm steel flats and
   Ø 15 mm steel rods
19 10 mm toughened glass sliding element in
   aluminium track
20 12 mm laminated construction board
   60/120 mm steel RHS
   80 mm thermal insulation
   350–410 mm existing brickwork
   15 mm plaster
21 12 mm laminated construction board
   140 mm thermal insulation
   16 mm cement-bonded chipboard
22 15 mm laminated construction board on
   24 mm wood boarding
   80/171 mm timber joists and
   steel I-beams 120 mm deep
   80/30 mm battens; 30 mm thermal insulation
   12 mm perforated laminated
   construction board
23 6 mm sheet-steel covering bent to shape
24 reinforced concrete plinth, trowelled smooth

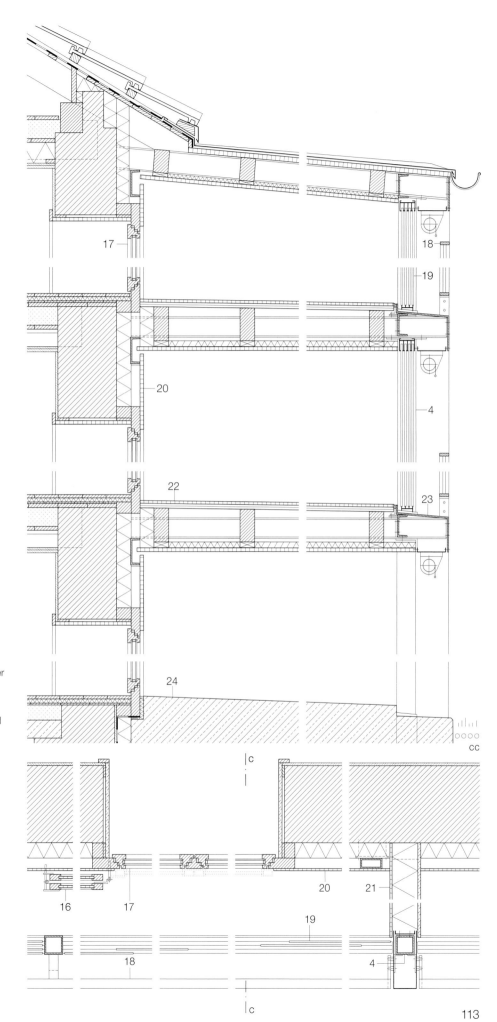

Insurance Building in Munich

Architects: Baumschlager & Eberle, Vaduz

Site plan   scale 1:4000

1 Administrative headquarters in
   building dating from 1913
2 Office building erected in 1973;
   converted and extended in 2002

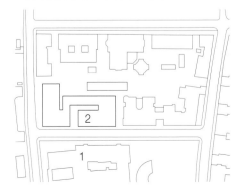

By day, the scale-like glazed facade of this office building shimmers in a green tone, reflecting the headquarters of the Munich reinsurance company opposite. The latter was erected in 1913 in what is now a historical district of the city. Today, it is a listed structure. The neighbourhood is distinguished by developments dating from the end of the 19th century, with rear courtyards that open on to the street.

Between all the fine surrounding buildings with their stucco facades stands what seems to be a new building. Without knowing its history, one would scarcely imagine it to be a typical 1970s structure erected shortly before the oil crisis, for it has undergone a complete conversion. At the time of its erection, little attention was paid to environmental and urban planning considerations. Designed by the Munich architects Maurer, Denk and Mauder for the reinsurance company, the building was originally to have been leased out, but during the construction stage, the clients realized that the office space in their old headquarters opposite was no longer adequate. They therefore decided to use the new development themselves. This five-floor office strip was raised one storey above the ground in part, and an aluminium bridge was spanned across the road, forging a direct link between the two buildings. With its elongated form and external exposed-aggregate concrete slab facings, the new structure created a clear contrast to other developments in the neighbourhood. At the beginning of 1998, after 25 years, a comprehensive survey of the building seemed necessary in terms of the general workplace situation and environmental standards. The tight, dark corridors and offices were the outcome of a functional space-saving division of the available areas, and the building no longer provided an adequate modern working environment. In addition, the office complex was uneconomical and cost-intensive in respect of present-day energy standards. The insurance company therefore decided in favour of a complete conversion.

Of the ten practices invited to participate in the architectural competition, Baumschlager and Eberle submitted the most convincing design. An incision was made in the long linear tract, and the scheme sought to adopt the proportions of the neighbouring developments. Instead of complete demolition and new construction, the architects proposed recycling the carcass and converting the complex in a model form. More than 50 per cent of the existing building volume was reused, including the load-bearing structure and the basement storeys. Floor areas were cut out, and the dark central zone of the three-bay reinforced concrete strip was converted into an open, L-shaped courtyard. The remaining concrete floor areas provide useful thermal-storage mass and have been integrated

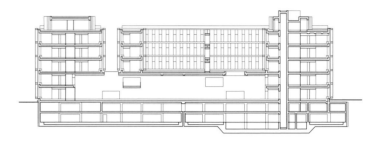

into the comprehensive new services and air-conditioning concept. The building now consumes only a quarter of the energy
it required in its previous state. The former top storey has been
replaced with two small organically shaped structures on the
roof, which are set back slightly from the facade and house
conference rooms and executive offices. The aluminium bridge
has been removed and replaced by a tunnel that extends to
the headquarters building. Light installations by Keith Sonnier
and James Turrell enhance the quality of the basement corridors that link up the insurance concern's other buildings scat-
tered over the entire neighbourhood. An additional L-shaped
structure was added to the south of the existing building,
emphasizing the corner situation. The complex, including the
load-bearing structure, has been extended in depth by a quarter. Although it was not possible to change the grid dimension
of 1.87 m, the working conditions in the unit offices have been
considerably improved. Visual links to the outside world and to
the moss-lined courtyard create a pleasant working environment. By installing translucent divisions between the offices
and the corridors and increasing the transparent area of the
facade to 80 per cent, the natural lighting conditions have
been greatly enhanced. The double-skin glazed facade forms
an integral part of the low-energy concept. The external layer,
consisting of fixed panes of laminated safety glass set on the
rake, is supported by projecting cornice strips that articulate
the facade horizontally at the level of the internal upstand
walls. The inner facade skin comprises a three-layer low-E
glass-and-aluminium construction with motor-operated opening lights that can be individually controlled.
As with the design of the tunnels, artists were involved in the
conversion measures from the very outset. In the entrance hall,
a recess in the wall opens once an hour, revealing motifs from
nature on otherwise concealed screens. With an artistic wall
design, it was possible to overcome the sense of constriction
in the staircase spaces. Olafur Eliasson created a distinctive
wall of moss in the entrance and also designed a nocturnal
facade installation, consisting of vertical bands of light. The
electricity for this is generated by a photovoltaic plant on the
roof. The visually dominant materials – aluminium, stainless
steel, glass, maple and Anröchte dolomite – are used to great
effect to highlight various sections of the building. The multi-
purpose entrance hall, for example, is clad entirely in small-
scale maple parquet and shimmers in reddish-brown tones,
while the courtyard is enlivened by a grove of North American
maple trees. In the autumn, the brilliant colours of their leaves
give the employees of the Munich reinsurance concern a taste
of an Indian summer.

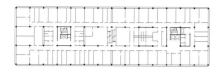

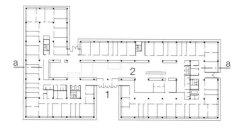

1 Entrance
2 Entrance hall
3 Courtyard
4 Board rooms
5 Conference room

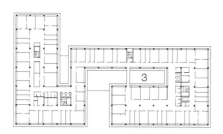

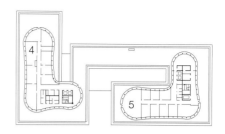

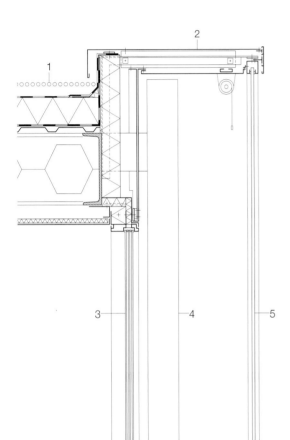

Vertical section   scale 1:20

1 roof construction (board rooms):
   80 mm planted layer
   protective matting
   root-resisting sheeting
   plastic-modified bituminous
   sealing layer
   140 mm polyurethane thermal
   insulation
   vapour barrier
   trapezoidal-section ribbed metal
   sheeting 35 mm deep laid to falls
   on sheet metal
   castellated beam 390 mm deep
   suspended soffit 95 mm deep
2 3 mm black-red-anodized sheet
   aluminium covering with anti-
   drumming coating
3 triple low-E glazing: 3× 6 mm
   glass and 2× 12 mm cavities
4 Ø 168.3/6.3 mm tubular steel
   column
5 15 mm toughened safety glass
6 60 mm gravel alternating with
   60 mm Bärlach sandstone slabs

140 mm special substrate
layer
15 mm granular-rubber mat
root-resisting sheeting
plastic-modified bituminous
sealing layer
140 mm polyurethane
thermal insulation
vapour barrier
90 mm concrete topping
finished to falls
7 21 mm laminated safety
   glass balustrade with
   stainless-steel handrail
8 600/175 mm Anröchte
   dolomite with 2× Ø 76/5 mm
   stainless-steel anchor pieces
   per element glued in
9 laminated safety glass:
   2× 12 mm partially
   toughened glass
10 fabric sunblind
11 thermal separation
   of bracket

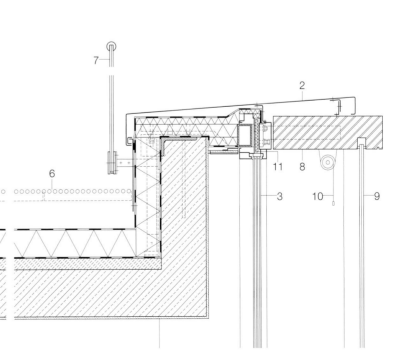

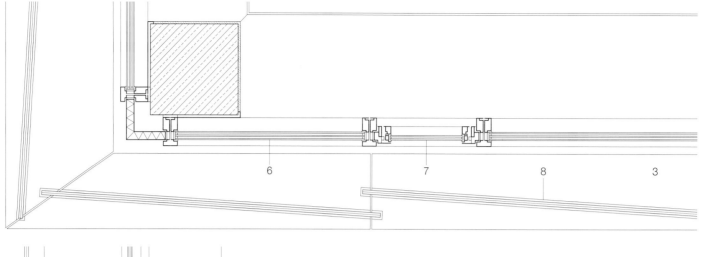

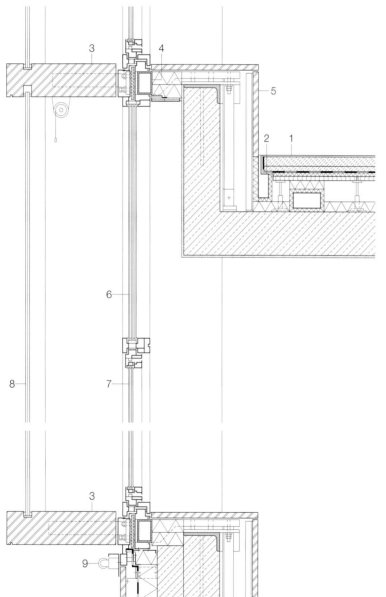

1 office floor construction:
  8 mm Canadian maple strip
  parquet
  58 mm anhydrite screed
  heating/cooling system in
  30 mm nubbed slabs
  20 mm impact-sound insulation
  22 mm bearing sheet over
  167 mm floor cavity
  50 mm insulation
  230 mm existing reinforced
  concrete floor with
  plastered soffit
2 fresh-air inlet
3 600/175 mm Anröchte dolomite
  with 2× Ø 76/5 mm stainless-
  steel anchor pieces per element
  glued in

5 30 mm Anröchte dolomite
4 120/80/4 mm galvanized
  steel RHS bracing to
  facade element with
  2× 40 mm steel flat fixings
6 facade elements:
  black-red-anodized alu-
  minium with triple low-E
  glazing: 3× 6 mm glass
  and 2× 12 mm cavities
7 double glazing
  (6 + 14 + 6 mm)
8 laminated safety glass:
  2× 12 mm partially
  toughened glass; corner
  elements: 15 + 12 mm
9 moisture-proof lighting strip
10 40 mm Anröchte dolomite

1 wall construction in corridor:
   Canadian maple strip veneer on
   15 mm birch plywood; with Ø 4 mm
   perforations; protective matting
   20 mm rock wool between
   40/20 mm bearers
   2× 12.5 mm plasterboard
   50 mm rock wool between
   50 mm studding
   2× 12.5 mm plasterboard
2 soffit construction:
   Canadian maple strip veneer on
   15 mm birch plywood; with Ø 4 mm
   perforations; protective matting
   60 mm rock-wool insulation between
   60/60 mm wood framing
3 fluorescent tube
4 sheet-steel division
5 air extract

6 sprinkler
7 inspection opening
8 lamp with integral air-extract opening
9 glazed partition: 6 + 8 mm glass +
   88 mm cavity
10 hall floor construction: 8 mm Canadian
   maple strip parquet
   58 mm anhydrite screed
   30 mm heating-/cooling-system
   floor slabs in area near facade on
   separating layer
   20 mm impact-sound insulation
   22 mm bearing sheet over
   167 mm floor cavity
   50 mm rock-wool insulation with
   foil coating
   230 mm existing reinforced concrete floor
11 insulation block with plasterboard on
   both faces

Horizontal and
vertical sections
through facade
Vertical section
through corridor
scale 1:20

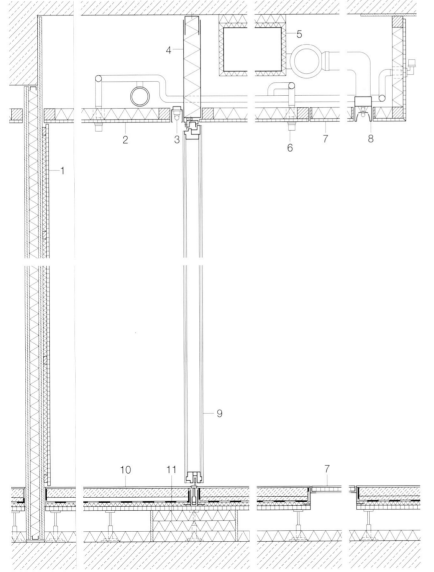

Section through entrance hall   scale 1:50

1 moss-covered tuff stones
   roof sealing layer; thermal insulation; vapour barrier
   230 mm existing concrete slab
   bearers with acoustic insulation
   strip parquet soffit lining with pinhole perforations
2 roof light: 10 + 6 + 16 mm glass and
   2× 13 mm cavities
3 airtight seal on three sides
4 ceiling light with tensioned plastic covering
5 fire-compartment roller shutter
6 balustrade: 20 mm laminated safety glass
7 wall construction: strip parquet on 20 mm composite wood
   acoustic element; 30 mm mineral wool; polythene sheeting;
   60/80 mm timber studding
   plasterboard stud wall (1/2 hr. fire resistance)
   cupboard with boarding and strip parquet
8 72 mm sliding fire division

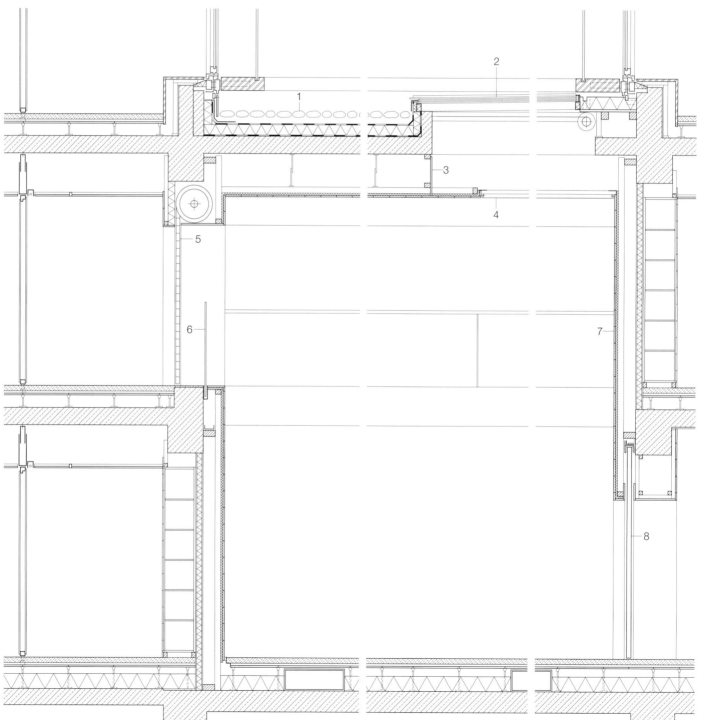

Alf Lechner Museum in Ingolstadt

Architects: Fischer Architects, Munich

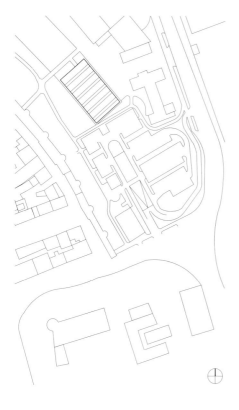

Visitors to this former industrial building are welcomed in the gravel forecourt by a sculpture. Situated close to the old city centre, the hall, with a north-light roof structure, dates from the 1950s and was in a desolate state of repair prior to its conversion. Forming part of an extensive factory site, it was originally used for car and motorcycle production and later served as a vehicle hall, canteen, costume store and rehearsal stage. After its acquisition by a museum foundation, the building was transformed with simple means into an elegant gallery. Today, it is a unique and clearly articulated location for art, housing the works of the steel sculptor Alf Lechner.

As a result of the various functions the building had accommodated in the course of its life, the interior was cluttered with numerous installations and fittings, so that it was necessary initially to strip the hall down to its carcass structure. An exhibition area of 1,000 m² has been created on the ground floor for large-scale sculpture, with a further area of about 800 m² on the upper floor, which houses smaller sculptural works and drawings and a number of ancillary spaces.

Approaching the museum from the north, visitors have direct access to the exhibition area via a steel entrance portal. On this side, the gallery opens like a display window: a roughly two-metre-deep vestibule in steel and glass forms a striking contrast to the otherwise closed facades and affords a view of the exhibition within. Economic constraints prevented the architects realizing their proposal for a formal stairway in this two-storey projecting structure. The vertical circulation is concealed within internal staircase spaces.

On the other three faces, the building has a new attire, consisting of gleaming matt-silver aluminium cladding riveted on, with carefully laid out joints. The aluminium sandwich panels are crisply mitred at the corners of the building. The rainwater pipes that drain the north-light roofs are housed in the 25 cm ventilated cavity to the rear of this cladding. The joints around the requisite doors and gates are barely visible in the metal skin, while the ventilation and window openings to the ancillary spaces are completely concealed behind perforated aluminium sheeting. Nothing interrupts the continuity of the skin and the clear lines of the building volume. An unusual solution was chosen for the heating. Concealed pipes in the external walls at plinth level heat the solid structure, which forms part of a thermoactive system. In consultation with the local authorities, it was possible to omit insulation in the outer walls. It was, however, incorporated in the roofs, where the coverings and north-light glazing were renewed. The striking appearance of this structure is accentuated by the saw-tooth profile of the roof over the long rectangular form of the facades.

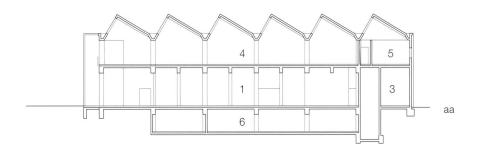

aa

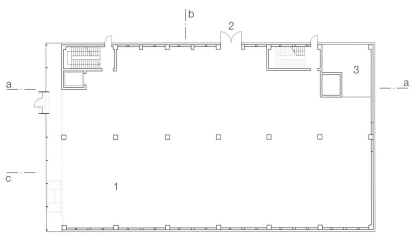

Site plan
scale 1:3000
Section · Floor plan
scale 1:500

1 Large-scale sculpture
2 Deliveries
3 Art store
4 Smaller sculpture and
  graphic art
5 Administration
6 Workshop

Vertical section through external wall
scale 1:10

1 plastic sealing layer to
  north-light roof
2 existing rainwater pipe
3 aluminium sandwich slab
4 extruded aluminium section
5 extruded aluminium intermediate
  section
6 aluminium T-section
7 existing window closed off
8 Ø 18/1 mm copper heating pipe

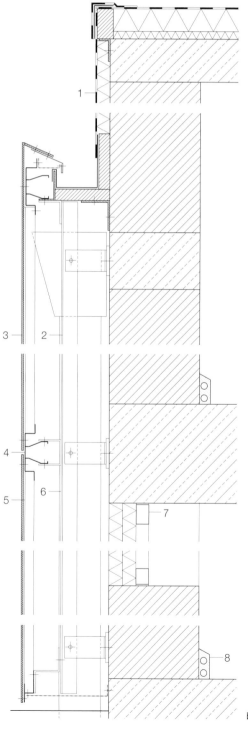

b

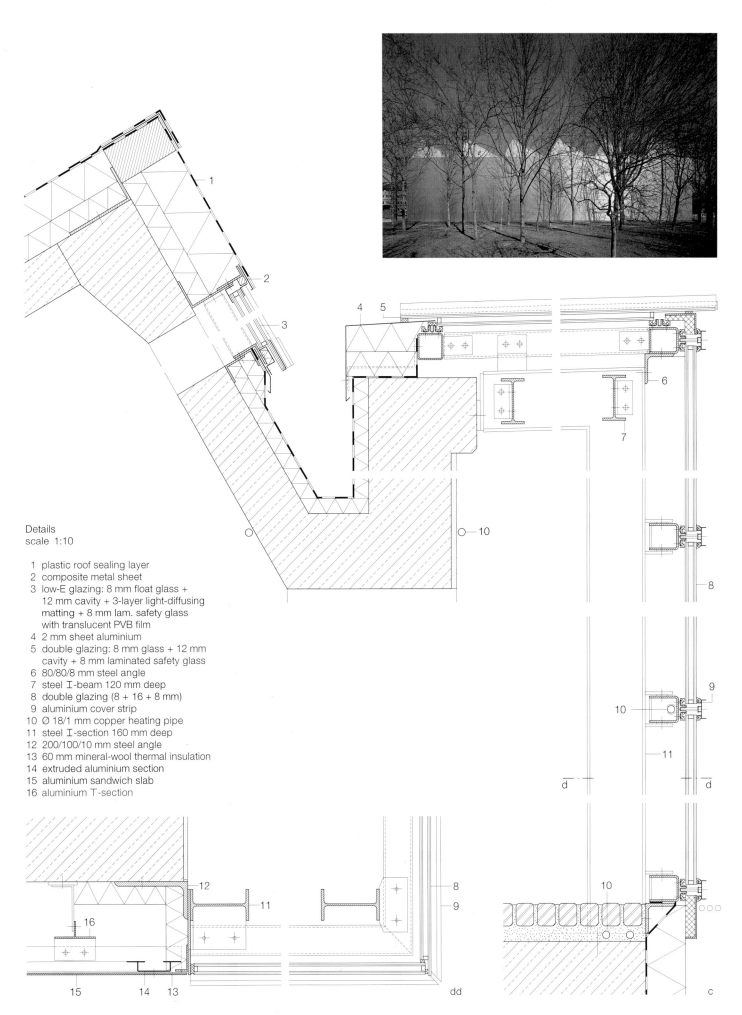

Details
scale 1:10

1 plastic roof sealing layer
2 composite metal sheet
3 low-E glazing: 8 mm float glass +
  12 mm cavity + 3-layer light-diffusing
  matting + 8 mm lam. safety glass
  with translucent PVB film
4 2 mm sheet aluminium
5 double glazing: 8 mm glass + 12 mm
  cavity + 8 mm laminated safety glass
6 80/80/8 mm steel angle
7 steel I-beam 120 mm deep
8 double glazing (8 + 16 + 8 mm)
9 aluminium cover strip
10 Ø 18/1 mm copper heating pipe
11 steel I-section 160 mm deep
12 200/100/10 mm steel angle
13 60 mm mineral-wool thermal insulation
14 extruded aluminium section
15 aluminium sandwich slab
16 aluminium T-section

MoMA QNS in New York

Architects: Michael Maltzan architecture, Los Angeles
Cooper, Robertson & Partners, New York

The Museum of Modern Art (MoMA), founded in 1929, has out-grown its spatial capacity – and not for the first time in its history. The complex of buildings in Midtown Manhattan, which has been in use since 1939, is undergoing a programme of conversion and extension designed by Yoshio Taniguchi. These measures, which are scheduled to last from 2002 to 2005, will double the floor area of the museum. In view of the fruitless search for alternative quarters in Manhattan for the period of the construction work, a decision was made to move the museum temporarily to a hall in Queens. The new location lies between the city centre and the suburbs in an area full of commercial uses, workshops, warehouses, garages and parking lots. The museum's temporary quarters, which bear the name MoMA QNS are situated in a former staples factory, which was originally acquired by MoMA as a depot.

The conversion of the factory was divided between two practices. Cooper Robertson & Partners designed the gallery spaces and the administration and research tract, while Michael Maltzan was responsible for the outer appearance and the sequence of entrance spaces.

Most visitors arrive by the elevated subway, so that the first facade they see is the roof of the building. Fragments of the MoMA logo have been painted on the technical roof structures in such a way that they coalesce to form the full insignia shortly before trains enter the station. A long strip of fluorescent light tubes leads the way along the building – painted in a vivid blue colour – to the entrance. A white plinth band accentuates the horizontal lines of the flat, box-like structure. Internally, a staircase and ramp lead to the ticket counter, beyond which is a "project space" for special exhibitions.

The lobby is flanked by further ramps that lead to a gallery level with a café and shop. At this point, the rectilinear volume is disrupted, and the space can be experienced in a variety of forms. Changing perspectives and glimpses of the adjoining galleries catch the eyes of visitors. The simple detailing and materials, such as screeded floors, are in keeping with the industrial character of the building. The black-painted ceiling, bearing various unclad service installations, recedes visually to the point where it is scarcely perceptible. Similarly restrained in appearance are the exhibition areas, which are situated in a large hall that can be flexibly divided into a number of spaces. Art enjoys precedence here, and visitors can experience it in a more immediate form than in the cultivated surroundings of the headquarters building. After the reopening of the Manhattan complex, MoMA QNS will continue to operate as a depot and research institute. To what extent it will then function as a museum still has to be decided.

Site plan
scale 1:10,000

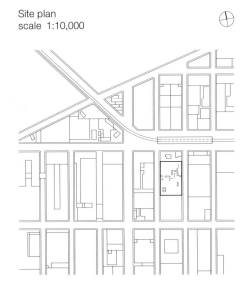

Ticket counter and space
for special exhibitions
Section   scale 1:20

1 roof construction (refurbished):
   two-layer bituminous sealing membrane
   rigid-foam thermal insulation
   thermal insulation to falls
   vapour barrier
   12.7 mm plasterboard
   38 mm existing ribbed metal sheeting
2 existing steel I-beam 305 mm deep
3 254 mm steel channel section
4 152 mm steel channel section
5 92 mm steel channel section
6 2× 16 mm plasterboard
7 16 mm plasterboard
   13 mm plywood
8 steel I-beam 457 mm deep
9 102/38 mm steel RHS handrail
10 13 mm perspex balustrade
11 floor screed
12 steel I-beam 254 mm deep
13 38 mm steel channel section
14 Ø 152/6 mm tubular steel column
15 Ø 70 mm steel tube
16 2× 19 mm medium-density fibreboard

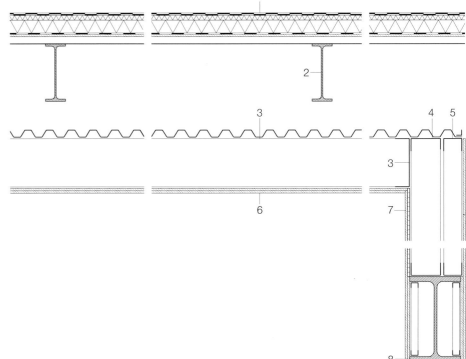

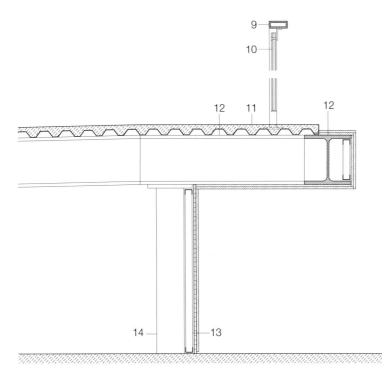

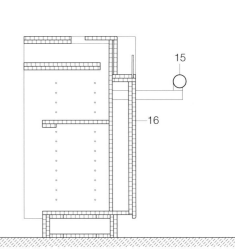

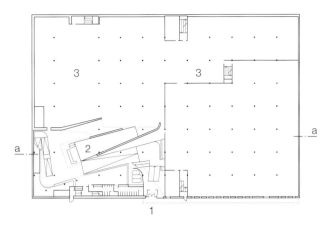

Floor plans · Section
scale 1:1250

1 Entrance
2 Project space
3 Exhibition space
4 Café/Shop

Tate Modern in London

Architects: Herzog & de Meuron, Basle

Externally, this huge brick structure has scarcely changed. Apart from the streams of visitors who cross the bridge over the Thames every day on their way to this imposing edifice, the only outward sign of its new function is the long glass box on the roof. At night, it radiates light into the sky over London; by day, it allows daylight to enter the gallery spaces below. The large lettering on its face also serves to inform the public over a great distance about the exhibitions in the gallery. Designed by Sir Giles Gilbert Scott, the creator of the famous red telephone boxes, the building was formerly one of the largest power stations in Britain. It was erected between 1947 and 1963 in Southwark, one of the poorer boroughs of London, establishing a close juxtaposition between industry and housing in the capital. The smokestack, which polluted the air of the city centre for decades, was not allowed to rise above the height of the dome of St Paul's Cathedral on the other side of the river. Although neither the form nor the central position of the 93-metre stack was dictated by functional needs, the chimney acts as a vertical articulating element in the middle of the complex. This clearly structured brick colossus thus entered into a dialogue with the dome of the cathedral. The power station was organized in three parallel linear tracts. Facing the Thames was the boiler house; in the middle was the hall with the great turbines; and along the south side was the transformer plant that once provided much of London with electricity. The transformers still stand there today. Thirteen years after the closure of the power station in 1981, a competition was held for the transformation of this industrial monument into the Tate Modern – the fourth such gallery after the Tate Britain, the Tate Liverpool and the Tate in St Ives. The competition was won by Herzog and de Meuron, and in 2000, after a three-year construction period, the gallery was inaugurated. Although the interior was virtually gutted, the architects managed to retain the special character of this powerful building, including its three-part division. Contrasted with the existing structure, with its terse, vertical window slits, the illuminated glass strip on the roof is an expression of a new architectural approach in this scheme which is distinguished by a sense of clarity and consistency. Outside the building, a broad, steep ramp burrows its way into the ground, marking the west facade as the main entrance front. The ramp leads into the former turbine hall, which now serves as a public concourse and a space for the presentation of unusual works of art. Almost 160 metres long and 30 metres high, the hall extends over the entire length and height of the building. This vast space is dissected in the middle by a bridge, which is all that remains of a floor slab that originally stretched over the full length of the

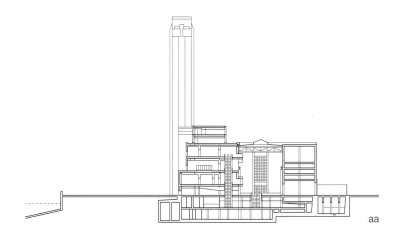

aa

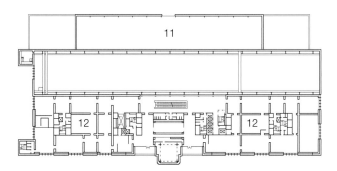

building. The bridge now provides access to the various exhibition levels in the former boiler house, linking them with the southern tract, which will be developed at a later date. The south side of the hall, with a riveted steel skeleton-frame structure, is closed, whereas on the other side of the concourse, visitors enjoy views into the exhibition areas through projecting, glazed linear strips or "bay windows". These illuminated volumes seem to hover in the hall space, interrupting the vertical lines of the steel piers and exhibiting the visitors who may be standing there, as if in a showcase. Two existing assembly gantries have been restored and are now used to lift heavy works of art into the adjoining gallery spaces. The roughly 14,000 m² exhibition areas are spread over three storeys and are divided into spaces of different dimensions and proportions to accommodate the needs of various exhibits. The works of art date from 1900 to the present day and are organized in four thematic groups, with landscape, still life, nude and history sections – an unusual form of presentation that is not arranged chronologically nor according to specific periods. Daylight enters via the huge windows and is complemented by finely adjustable lighting strips let into the plasterboard soffits. In their design and in the intensity of the illumination they provide, these strips are scarcely distinguishable from the roof lights on the third gallery level. Shiny grey cement-and-sand screeding was used in most areas of the building, with the exception of the exhibition spaces, where the flooring consists of untreated oak parquet with cast-iron gratings for the fresh-air inlets. The shimmering green glass strip at the top of the building houses mechanical services, and a restaurant that affords a view over the skyline of London – over the Thames and Foster's new Millennium Bridge to St Paul's Cathedral.

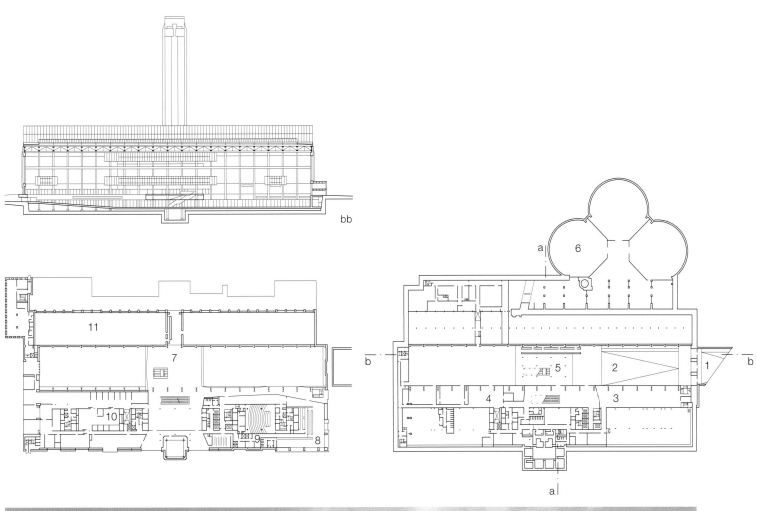

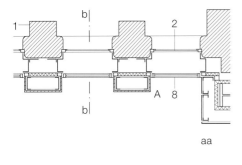

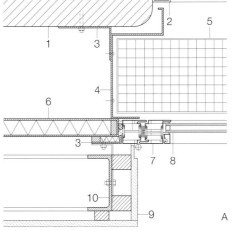

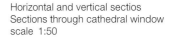

aa

A

bb

ā   ā

2

8

B

C

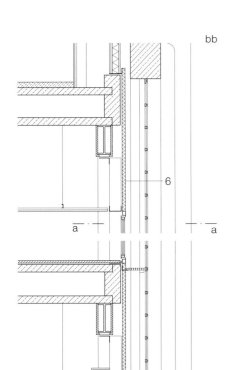

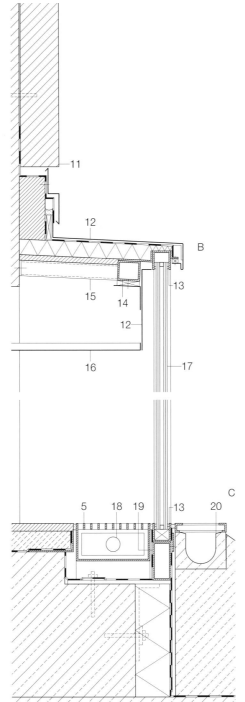

B

11

12

13

15   14

12

16   17

5   18   19   13   20

C

Horizontal and vertical sectios
Sections through cathedral window
scale 1:50

Details
scale 1:10

1 existing brickwork
2 existing steel window
3 3 mm sheet steel bent to shape
4 2 mm sheet steel bent to shape
5 steel grating
6 45 mm insulated sheet-steel panel
7 steel casement and frame
8 24 mm double glazing
9 plasterboard
10 150 mm steel channel section
11 100 mm suspended brick facing skin
12 2 mm sheet-aluminium covering bent
      to shape
13 50/50/4 mm steel channel section
14 60/50/3 mm steel RHS
15 40/40/3 mm steel SHS
16 sheet-steel suspended soffit
17 32 mm double glazing:
      2× laminated safety glass
18 convector heater
19 100/50/3 mm steel RHS welded to
      250/10 mm steel plate
20 prefabricated drainage channel with
      steel cover grating

Galleries
ᴵ⁰ &wc ↗

Tate Modern: Collection 2000
in association with BT

The Unilever Series: Louise Bourgeois
Sponsored by Unilever U

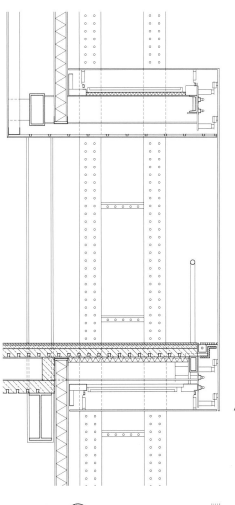

Balcony in turbine hall
scale 1:50
Sectional details scale 1:10

1 22 mm lam. safety glass with
sandblasted outer face and
opal epoxy-resin-coated
inner face
2 sliding element:
13 mm lam. safety glass
with sandblasted outer face
3 Ø 68 mm aluminium tube
4 12 mm steel plate
5 fluorescent tube
6 310 mm steel channel section
7 80/80/6 mm steel SHS
8 50/50/6 mm steel SHS with
130/10 mm steel plate welded on
9 75/50/46 mm milled
steel element
10 200/100/5 mm steel RHS
11 45 mm insulated
aluminium panel
12 metal grating
13 heating pipe
14 Ø 60 mm tubular steel
balustrade post
15 Ø 60 mm tubular steel handrail
16 floor construction
12 mm untreated oak parquet
18 mm plywood
50 mm cement-and-sand screed
110 mm concrete filigree floor

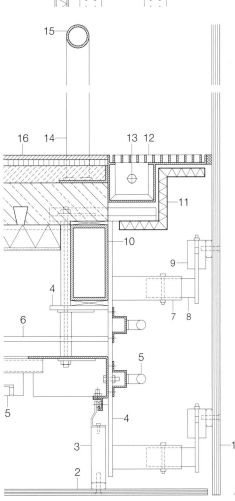

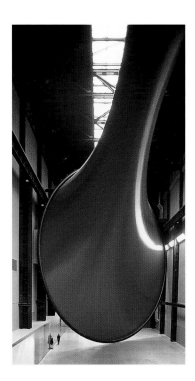

Cultural and Business Centre in Turin

Architects: Renzo Piano Building Workshop, Genoa

The Lingotto is one of the landmarks of Turin. This huge factory, erected for Fiat at the beginning of the 1920s, was one of the largest automobile works in Europe and was long regarded as a symbol of the modernization of Italy. Today, the Lingotto, which literally means a "bar" or "block", accommodates a wide range of functions, including shops, offices, restaurants, university teaching spaces, cinemas, trade fair halls and a hotel, to mention but a few. In other words, it plays the role of a cultural, conference, shopping and educational centre, rather like a small town in its own right within the capital of Piedmont. A 26 × 60 m auditorium, sunk 16 m below the rest of the building on one side to save space, can be used for lectures or as a concert hall. It can be modified to create spaces of four different sizes, seating between 495 and 2,090 people.

Giovanni Agnelli founded the Fabbrica Italiana Automobili Torino in this city in 1899. In 1915, the company management decided to build the new factory and commissioned the engineer Giacomo Mattè Trucco to undertake the planning and execution of the work. By 1921, the main block had been completed. It consisted of two parallel strips more than 500 m long and 24 m wide linked by five short cross-tracts with goods lifts that served the continuous vertical manufacturing processes. The reinforced concrete structure was based on American models and on theories developed by Frederick Winslow Taylor for an efficient division of labour oriented to conveyor-belt systems and the vertical organization of production.

The facade design was determined not only by the structure of the building, but by its functional layout. Room-height windows, for example, ensured a maximum ingress of daylight. The vehicle production sequence proceeded storey by storey from the bottom to the top of the factory, culminating in the more than one-kilometre-long racing track on the roof, where the engineers tested new prototypes – a total of 80 different models over the years. The trial circuit specially laid out for this purpose is unique and is still the distinguishing feature of the Lingotto today. After the narrow tracts at the north and south ends had been completed with up and down ramps for the new cars, the factory was officially opened in 1926.

For more than 50 years, Fiat produced its vehicles in this huge building. During that time, the concern erected other, even larger industrial works and transferred much of the production

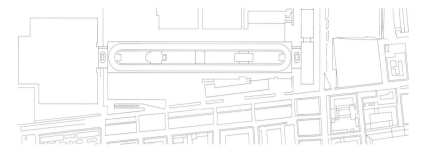

Site plan   scale 1:10,000

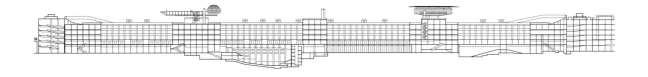

Section · Plan of roof   scale 1:4000

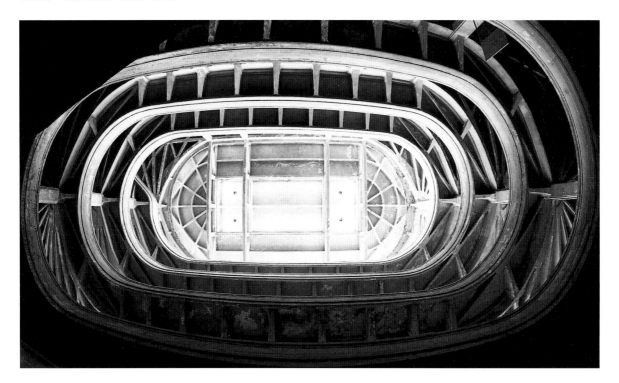

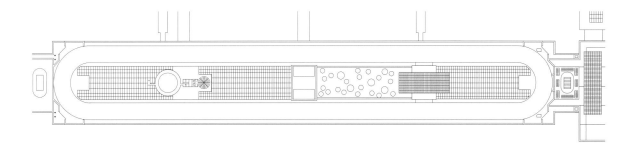

to new locations. Two years after the 1980 economic recession, the Lingotto was closed.

An international architectural competition for the conversion of this powerful industrial monument was won by Renzo Piano, who then undertook the restructuring and redesign of the complex. This was executed in three separate stages between 1991 and 2002. Each section of the conversion work was self-contained and fully functional on completion. The underlying aim of the rehabilitation was to bring out the original 1920s structure again. Subsequent additions were removed. Where the concrete columns were underdimensioned for the future use, they were either replaced with new ones increased in size.

The facades remained unchanged. It is the structures on the roof that dominate the new appearance of the building, however. The hemispherical glazed conference hall on the rooftop is linked with a helicopter landing pad; and in 2002, the "Scrigno" was created opposite, a small museum elevated above the city. The contents of this "shrine" were donated by Giovanni Agnelli, the grandson of the Fiat company founder. He bequeathed 25 works of art from his private collection to the city; and with this gallery, he created a striking monument to himself over the rooftops of Turin. Outwardly, the distinctive form of this museum, with its closed, windowless sheet-steel skin, conjures images of a structure with a technical function. Raised on four steel columns over the existing roof, it steals the show even from the former racing track. The main entrance to the museum, with an exhibition area of 450 m², is within the building on the level of the shopping centre. On request, however, visitors can be brought to the gallery by taxi via the southern access ramp and can even complete a lap on the rooftop track.

The works of art, which include paintings by Matisse, Picasso and Renoir as well as a number of sculptures, are illuminated by filtered top light. The broadly cantilevered roof recalls a structure the architect designed for the Fondation Beyeler near Basle. The lower layer consists of sheets of glass 2.12 × 4.50 m in size. The upper layer, which Piano describes as a "magic carpet", comprises roughly 1,800 glass louvres set diagonally in a three-dimensional steel grid which covers an area of 55 × 20 m. The structure is designed to screen off solar radiation, while ensuring optimum lighting conditions. The pictures are hung on free-standing cross-walls. The long side walls are not used. The museum forms a continuation of the exhibition areas in the southern section of the Lingotto, where the six gallery levels are linked by internal steel escalators and two panorama lifts that are visible on the outside of the building.

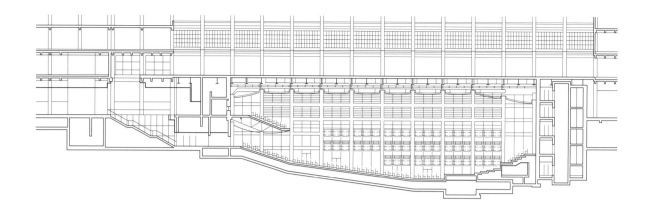

Section through auditorium
scale 1:750
Elevation of side wall
with acoustic elements
scale 1:100
Details of acoustic panel
scale 1:10

1 MDF acoustic panel with wood lining
  on both faces
2 cast-iron bracket, painted
3 adjustable steel strut, painted
4 veneered wood lining
5 steel balustrade post, painted
6 carpeting

7 chipboard underfloor layer
8 reinforced concrete floor slab
9 steel anchor plate, painted
10 adjustable anchor element
11 steel track for acoustic elements,
   painted
12 plasterboard soffit

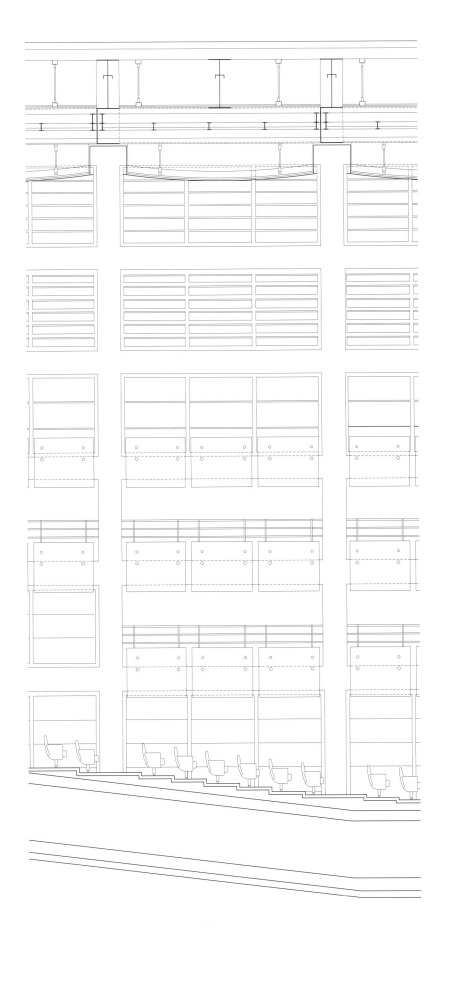

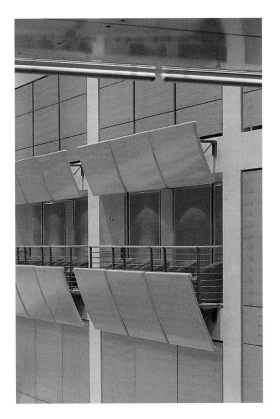

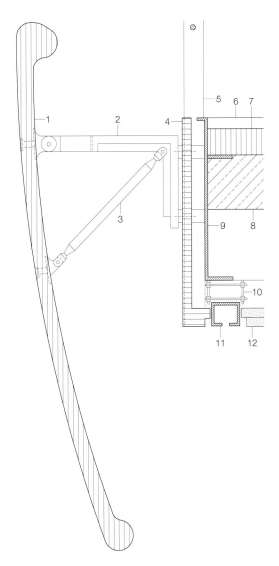

Gallery
Floor plan · Section
scale 1:400
Axonometric of
primary structure

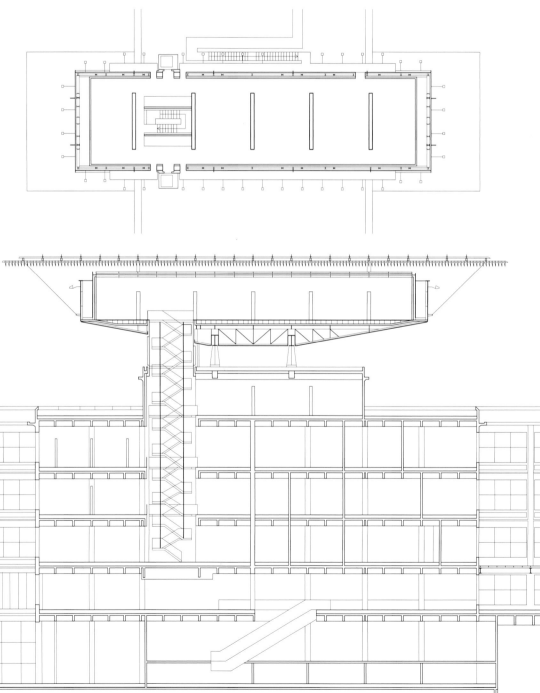

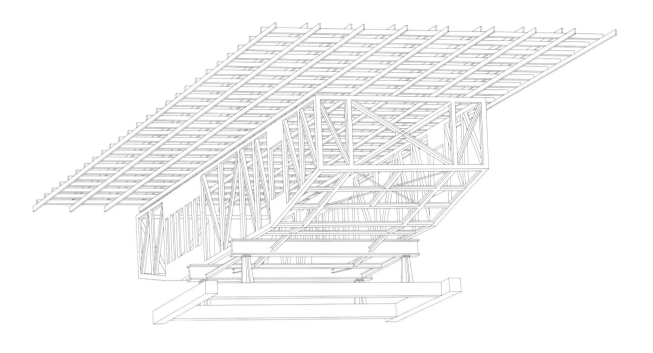

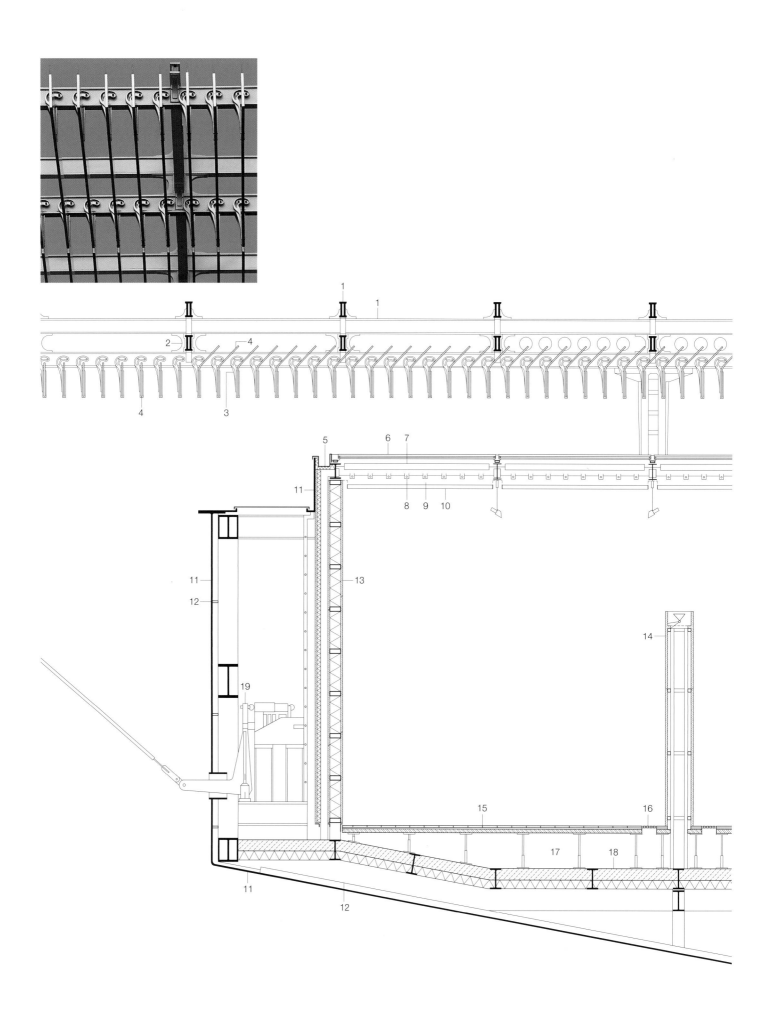

Sectional details of gallery
scale 1:50

1 100/200 steel section:
   18 mm steel plate, painted
2 cast-steel stiffening, sandblasted and painted
3 cast stainless-steel louvre fixings, polished
4 laminated glass louvre:
   2× 6 mm flint glass with milk-white PVB film
   and stainless-steel edge strip
5 sheet-copper gutter
6 double glazing: 24 mm lam. safety glass
   (2× 12 mm toughened flint glass)
   + 18 mm cavity
   + 14 mm lam. safety glass
   (6 + 8 mm toughened flint glass),

silicone bonded
7 pivoting aluminium louvre
8 fluorescent lighting tube
9 air-extract duct
10 9.00/1.97 m aluminium frame element
   with textile covering on both faces
11 12 mm sheet-steel outer casing, painted
12 reinforcing rib
13 4 mm glass-fibre-reinforced plastic sheeting
   2x 13 mm plasterboard
   150 mm rock-wool insulation
   2x 13 mm plasterboard
   100 mm air-extract duct

50 mm rock-wool insulation
   2x 13 mm plasterboard
14 4 mm glass-fibre-reinforced plastic sheeting
   2x 13 mm plasterboard
15 25 mm oak parquet
   20 mm softboard
   50 mm fibre-cement sheeting
16 oak grating
17 air-supply duct
18 150 mm concrete
   on ribbed metal sheeting
   120 mm insulation
19 tensioning device for stays

Documentation Centre in the Reichs Party Congress Complex in Nuremberg

Architect: Günther Domenig, Graz

Only when one stands on the arrow-like structure, walks through it, sees and almost feels how the metal cuts through the stone does one apprehend what the architect Günther Domenig means when he speaks of driving a stake through the flesh of the building. This steel member, which greets visitors at the entrance, cuts diagonally through the northern tract of the unfinished Congress Hall on the Reichs party convention site in Nuremberg.

Planned for the five National Socialist party congresses held between 1933 and 1939, the complex originally covered an area of roughly 20 hectares. According to Albert Speer's master plan, various monumental structures were to be erected for the mass gatherings of the Nazis. In addition to the Congress Hall, the Luitpold Arena, the Zeppelinfeld with a large grandstand, and the Märzfeld, this gigantic project also included a German Stadium – the "largest stadium in the world" – which was to provide space for 400,000 people. Today, most of the buildings have been destroyed or stripped down. The Congress Hall, however, which was meant to accommodate 50,000 people during the party conventions, remains the largest surviving building monument of the Nazi regime in Germany. The brick facade, clad with large granite slabs, radiates the coldness that is typical of the architecture of this era. Designed by Ludwig and Franz Ruff and modelled on the Colosseum in Rome, the building remained unfinished. It rises to a height of "only" 40 m instead of the planned 68 m. Although this derelict structure has been visibly exposed to decay, one senses the powerful, ominously impressive effect it still exerts.

With the location of the documentation centre in the northern tract of the main structure, the city of Nuremberg has set an important signal and faced up to its own past. In addition to a lecture hall, a cinema and a seminar tract, the centre houses an exhibition that focuses on the five Reichs party congresses held here. The exhibition route leads through the upper floor of the northern wing. The spaces have been left in their rough, unfinished state as far as possible to provide an appropriate setting for the didactic concept. The allusive game played here nevertheless blurs the sense of critical distance and deconstruction that the architecture conveys. The aim of the architectural treatment is evident from the outset. The end of the stake projects menacingly from the building at the entrance. The gash it inflicts is visible even externally. Situated above this gaping wound is the study forum, the angular shape of which adopts the same architectural language. Internally, too, the theme of disruption, dissection, laying bare is continued. The study forum, the projection hall and the exhibition space are all reached from the foyer,

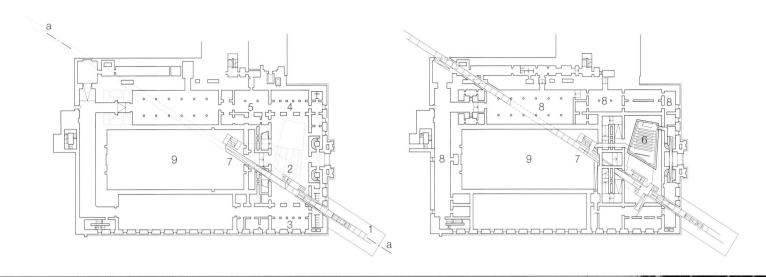

157

Longitudinal section through stake
scale 1:500

1 Entrance
2 Stake
3 Foyer
4 Exhibition space
5 Study forum
6 Courtyard of banners
7 Columned hall
8 External area

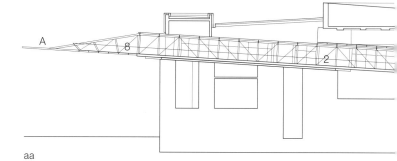

aa

through which the stake is driven on the diagonal. At the end of the exhibition route, visitors emerge from the building at the tip of the arrow, which has penetrated the masonry volume at this point and projects out 30 m above the level of the 150 × 160 m courtyard. On the way back to the foyer, one sees how the stake bores obliquely through the wounded body, disrupting the orthogonal grid. It shoots through the columned hall, planned as a vestibule for Hitler. Adroitly driven between the 12 five-metre-high pillars in Italian marble, it grazes them and thus robs them of their monumental effect. It crosses the court of banners and forces its way through walls that at some points are several metres thick. The mass of the masonry, the thousands of bricks concealed behind the stone-faced facade are made visible – a symbol of the Nazi regime's world of illusion.

Domenig uses raw, almost harsh, details. The old brickwork is left unclad. All internal fittings are in steel, and spatial enclosures are glazed as far as possible. The cladding is in gleaming aluminium. Even the asymmetric volume of the study forum is in these materials – with the exception of the floor slab, the raking wall elements and the soffit, which are in reinforced concrete. The stake or arrow is 130 metres long overall and consists of a steel-frame structure. At those points where it is not borne by the existing walls, it is supported by steel columns. The four steel beams that extend along its linear axis are connected by frame elements at 2.70 m centres. The fully glazed stake is dissolved at its ends. At the entrance, it assumes the form of a cantilevered canopy that ushers visitors into the documentation centre. At the other end of the route, the glass casing terminates at the point where visitors emerge into the courtyard space through two glazed doors.

The documentation centre is not a rehabilitation scheme in the conventional sense of that expression. A juxtaposition of old and new on equal terms would not have been possible here. This huge structure, with its historical overtones, has not been converted into a museum for exhibition purposes, therefore. It has been laid bare, almost dissected. The deconstructivist intervention can be seen as symbolic for a process of coming to terms with the past, with the Nazi architecture and the political, ideological system it represented. The destruction of the substance, the use of materials of cool, hard, austere appearance such as exposed concrete, sealed screeds and above all untreated steel and aluminium – all the things that reinforce the metaphor of a piercing arrow or a metal scalpel – reveal a treatment of the existing fabric that is not just a contrast, but a confrontation.

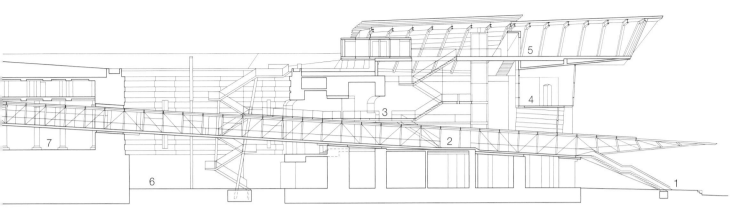

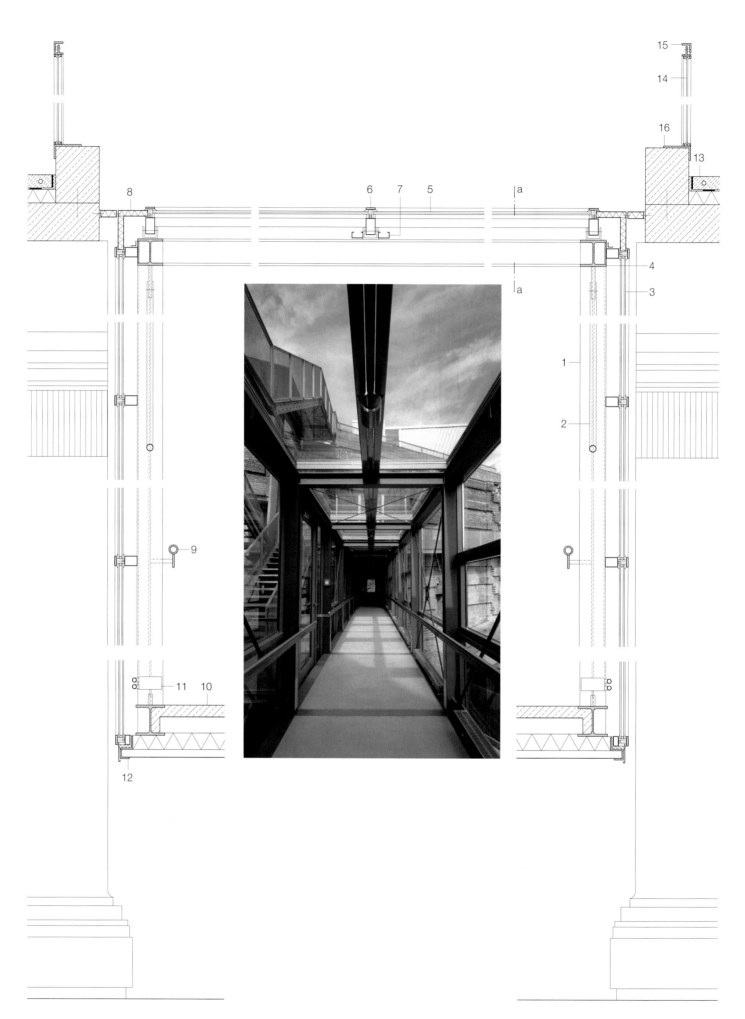

15

14

16

13

8

6 7 5

a

a

4

3

1

2

9

11 10

12

Sections through stake
Penetration of floor slab over columned hall
scale 1:20

1 steel frame: 4x I-beams 140 mm deep
2 Ø 35 mm steel tube
3 double glazing: 5 mm toughened glass
  + 6 mm cavity + 6 mm laminated safety glass
4 steel I-beam 140 mm deep
5 overhead glazing: laminated safety glass to
  bear foot traffic for cleaning
6 aluminium fixing strip in steel channel and
  fixed to load-bearing structure
7 steel channel cable duct
8 sheet-steel closing strip

9 Ø 42 mm stainless-steel
  tubular handrail welded
  to stainless-steel flat
10 floor construction:
  60 mm cement-and-sand screed, sealed
  ribbed metal sheeting 84 mm deep
  80 mm mineral-wool insulation
  corrugated aluminium sheeting
  35 mm deep
11 convector with point supports
12 50/50 mm steel angle

13 floor construction in exhibition space:
  70 mm screed around
  underfloor heating, sealed
  separating layer
  levelling layer on
  existing concrete floor slab
14 laminated safety glass balustrade:
  two layers of toughened glass
15 steel angle handrail
  fixed to steel T-section
16 150/7.5/7 mm steel angle

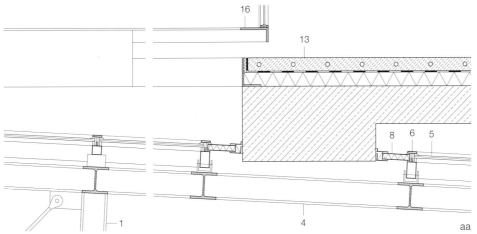

161

Longitudinal section through tip of stake A
Horizontal section
Plan
scale 1:20

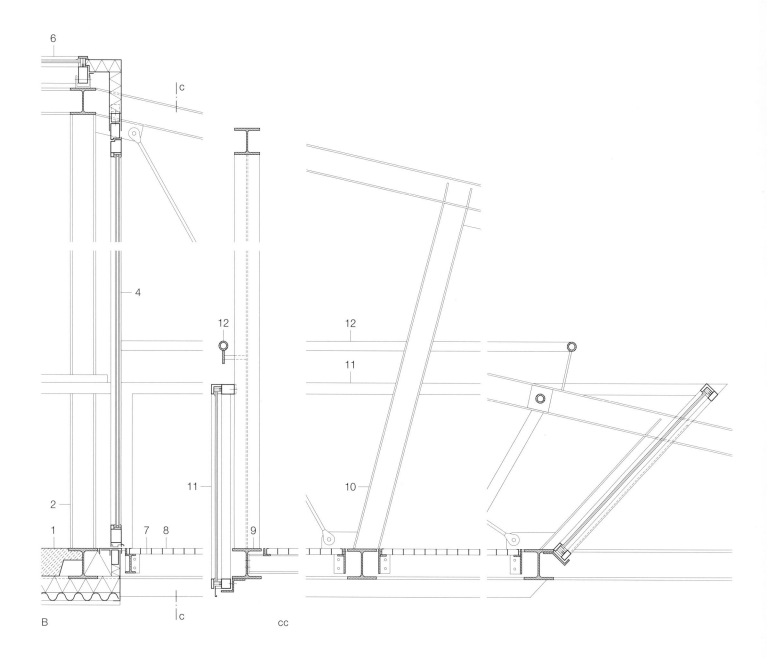

B

C

cc

C

B

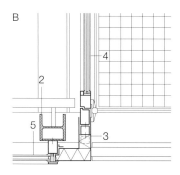

1 floor construction:
  60 mm cement-and-sand screed, sealed
  ribbed metal sheeting 84 mm deep
  80 mm mineral-wool insulation
  corrugated aluminium sheeting 35 mm deep
2 steel frame: 4x I-beams 140 mm deep
3 aluminium facade section
4 door with aluminium frame and double glazing
5 double glazing: 5 mm laminated safety glass +
  6 mm cavity + 6 mm toughened glass
6 overhead glazing: laminated safety glass to
  bear foot traffic for cleaning
7 continuous steel I-beam 140 mm deep

8 floor construction:
  metal grating (90/30 mm mesh) in
  35/35/5 mm steel angle frame
  secondary beam:
  steel I-section 100 mm deep
9 primary beam: steel I-section 140 mm deep
10 steel I-section 140 mm deep
11 continuous post-and-rail facade with
  laminated safety glass: 2x toughened glass
12 Ø 42 mm stainless-steel tubular handrail

All steel members galvanized

British Museum Courtyard in London

Architects: Foster and Partners, London

The British Museum, built by Sir Robert Smirke between 1823 and 1852, is one of the main tourist attractions of London. With its archaeological and ethnological collections from all over the world, the museum attracts more than five million visitors a year. For a long time, they all had to squeeze their way through a small entrance hall in the south side of this four-tract building and follow a labyrinthine route through the linear sequence of exhibition spaces. With the refurbishment of the courtyard, a generous circulation zone has been created from where visitors have easy access to the various galleries. This central space has been covered with a spectacular glass roof and now provides ample space for shops, cafés and other central functions.

Smirke's original plans envisaged the courtyard as a park-like planted area. Soon after its completion, however, it became a forgotten back yard. As early as 1857, Sydney Smirke, the architect's brother, had inserted a domed structure in the middle which served as the reading room of the British Library. In the course of time, extension buildings were added as stockrooms for books, and stores for other objects. Cluttered with these various structures, the courtyard was closed to the public. With the relocation of the British Library to new quarters in St Pancras in 1998, it became possible to open up the courtyard and rejuvenate it for visitors. After the removal of the various huts and other extraneous structures, the 6,700 m² area was made accessible again – with the circular reading room standing proudly in the middle. Laid out around it are two extensive staircase tracts that lead up to an elliptical intermediate level with a restaurant, from where guests can observe the activities in the courtyard below. Carved in the stone along the staircases are the names of donors. The African collection has found a new home in the extensive spaces that have been cleared in the basement, where there are also two auditoriums and a number of seminar rooms. The museum's limestone facades have been restored, and the south portico inside the courtyard has been reconstructed to old plans. As early as 1876, it had been removed to make room for an extension to the entrance hall.

The circular reading room, a finely dimensioned structure in iron, brick and papier mâché, is one of the oldest examples of iron construction in Britain and has remained virtually unchanged internally. Externally, a second skin of Spanish limestone was drawn round the circular structure. Concealed behind this outer layer are 20 new steel columns (filled with concrete for structural and fireproofing purposes) which support the double-curved glass roof. Since the hall does not stand precisely in the middle of the courtyard, the new roof

Site plan   scale 1:5000
Section   scale 1:1500

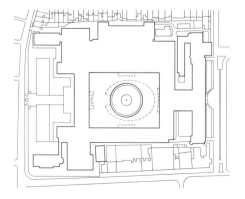

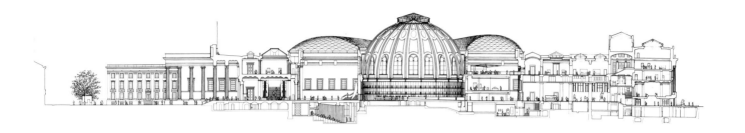

has a complex geometry – a torus stretched to a rectangular form. A special CAD program had to be developed to calculate the precise dimensions and the various angles of the individual roof elements. The roof has an average radius of about 50 m and becomes flatter towards the corners. In conjunction with the counter-curving spiralling elements, the radial RHSs spanning from the reading room to the walls of the museum form a lattice-shell structure. In the corners, where very high loads occur, the construction is reinforced by outer steel members. The lattice-shell form has the advantage of being rigid and self-supporting. As a result, only vertical loads are transmitted to the historical walls, and horizontal loading is reduced to a minimum. The elements of the steel structure were welded in the workshop and hoisted by cranes over the museum building. They were then laid on scaffolding that occupied the entire courtyard. To ensure optimum strength, the individual elements were welded together on site. Fifty-eight Teflon bearers on top of a reinforced concrete peripheral tie beam along the museum walls allow the structure to expand and contract by up to 50 mm. The roof is covered with 3,312 triangular panels of double-glazing, every one of which has a different form. Printed with a grid of white dots to filter out sunlight, the glazing elements form part of the largest internal courtyard covering in Europe. They were financed by private donors.

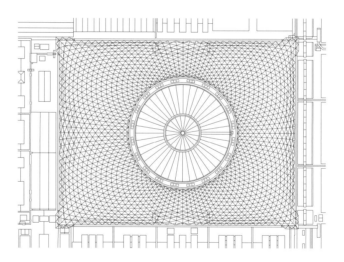

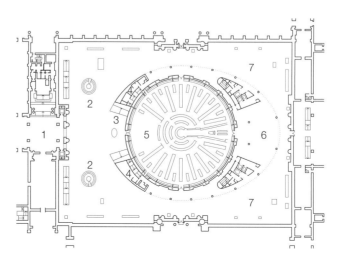

Plan of roof
Ground floor plan
scale 1:1500

1 Entrance
2 Information
3 Stairs to restaurant
4 WCs
5 Reading room
6 Shop
7 Café

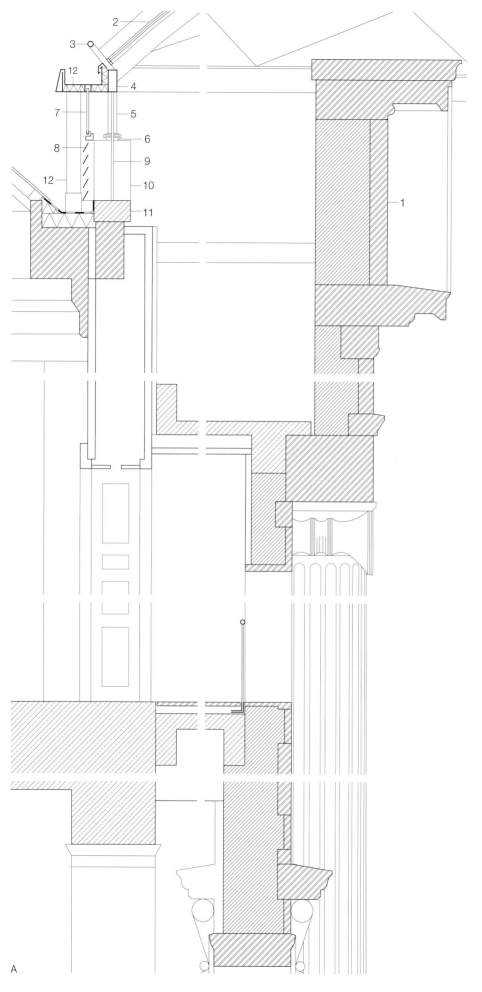

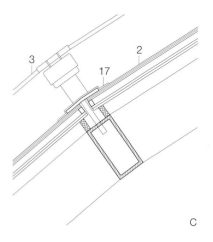

C

A Section through portico
B Section through courtyard facade
  scale 1:50
C Section through glazed roof
  scale 1:10

1 reconstructed limestone portico
2 glazed roof: 10 mm tinted toughened
   glass + 16 mm cavity + 10 mm
   laminated safety glass with 56%
   printed dotted grid as sunscreening
3 safety rail
4 150/350 mm steel RHS
5 120/120 mm steel SHS column
6 Teflon bearer
7 fixed glazing: 9 mm toughened glass

8 aluminium panels with opening louvres
9 Ø 27 mm steel bracing rod
10 reinforced concrete column
11 reinforced concrete peripheral tie beam
12 rainwater drainage
13 existing roof light
14 aluminium panel opening flap
15 sliding casement in wood frame
16 black-coated glazing
17 silicone sealing strip

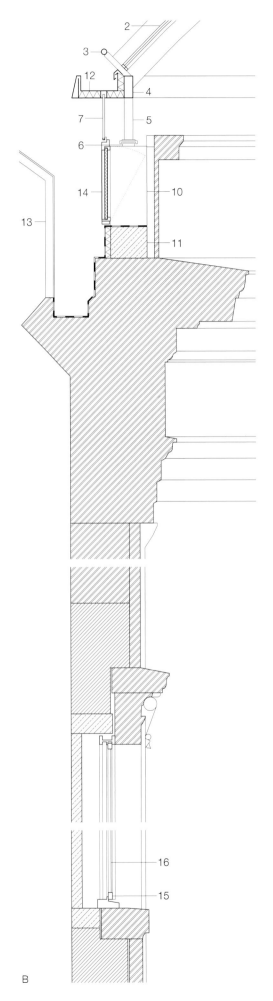

B

169

Reading room
Sectional details
scale 1:50

1 glazed roof:
   10 mm toughened glass
   + 16 mm cavity
   + 10 mm lam. safety glass
2 360/360 mm steel SHS tie beam
3 Ø 250 mm tubular steel column

4 fixed glazing: 9 mm
   toughened glass
5 fresh-air inlet
6 limestone cladding
7 ventilation duct
8 smoke curtain

9 existing window
10 existing masonry dome
11 air extract
12 plastic sealing layer on
   rigid-foam insulation
13 roof hatch

14 maintenance ladder
15 access platform:
   metal grating
16 Ø 457 mm tubular steel column
   filled with concrete
17 maintenance cradle for lighting

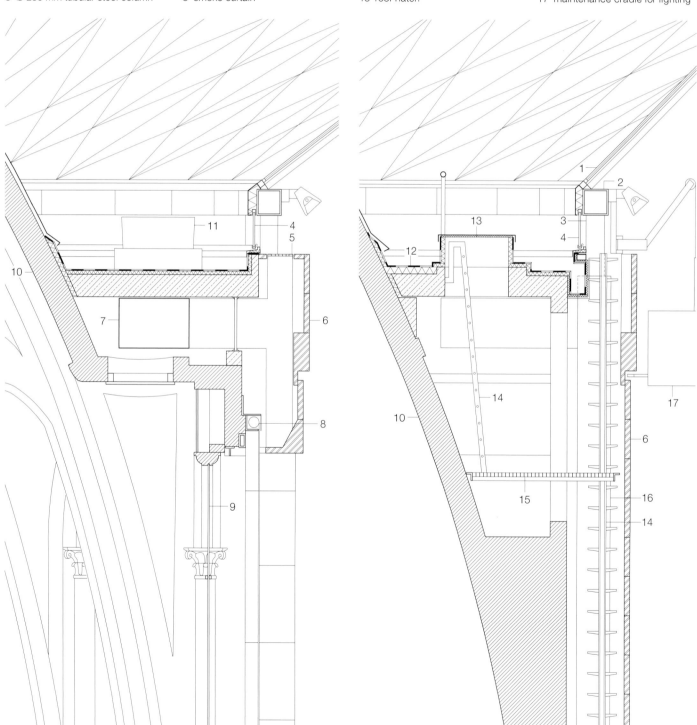

Urban Renewal in Salemi

Client:
Episcopal ordinariat
Mazara del Vallo, Italy
Architects:
Álvaro Siza Vieira, Porto
Roberto Collovà, Palermo
Associates:
Oreste Marrone, Viviana Trapani,
Ettore Tocco, Giambruno Ruggieri,
Francesca Tramonte, Ketti
Muscarella, Marco Ciaccio,
Guiseppe Malventano, Alba Lo
Sardo, Renato Viviano Architects,
Allessandro D'Amico, Pierangelo
Traballi, Angela Argento,
Melchiorre Armata
Structural planning (cathedral):
Sergio De Cola, Palermo
Completion: 1999

Álvaro Siza Vieira
Born 1933 in Matoshinhos,
Portugal; independent office in
Oporto; 1966–69 T.A. at the
University of Porto; since 1976
professor at the University of Porto.

www.alvarosiza.com

Museum in Colmenar Viejo

Client:
Municipality of Colmenar Viejo
Architects:
María José Aranguren Lopez, José
González Gallegos, Madrid
Associates:
Juan González Arce, Ignacio
Gonzalo Rosado, Luis Burriel
Bielza, Pablo Fernández Lewicki,
José Antonio Tallón Iglesias
Structural planning:
Ceider S. A.
Completion: 1998

María José Aranguren López
Born 1958 in Madrid; teaching
since 1984.

José González Gallegos
Born 1958 in Guadalajara,
Spain; teaching since 1984.

www.arangurengallegos.com

Visitor's Centre in Criewen

Client:
Land Brandenburg
Architects:
Anderhalten Architects, Berlin
Claus Anderhalten
Associates:
Christiane Giesenhagen, Sandra
Lorenz, Michael Schröder, Henning
von Wedemeyer
Supervision:
Hubertus Schwabe
Project supervision:
Landesbauamt Strausberg
Engineering:
Ingenieurbüro Rahn, Berlin
Structural planning:
AIP Ingenieurgesellschaft,
Schöneiche
Completion: 2000

Claus Anderhalten
Born 1962 in Cologne; associate in
the office of Peter Kulka; 1993
foundation of the office of
Anderhalten Architects in Berlin.

www.anderhalten.de

House and Studio Building in Sent

Client:
Private
Architects:
Rolf Furrer, Basle
Christof Rösch, Sent
Associates:
Simon Hartmann, Andreas
Hunkeler
Structural planning:
Andreas Zachmann, Basle
Completion: 2000

Rolf Furrer
Born 1955 in Basle; Switzerland;
since 1982 independent office in
Basle; since 2000 partnership with
Christof Rösch.

Christof Rösch
Born 1958 in Baden, Switzerland;
sculptor and architect/artist;
teaching at the College of Design in
Basle; since 2000 partnership with
Rolf Furrer.

r.furrer@architekten-bsa.ch

Cultural Centre in Toledo

Client:
The city of Toledo
Architect:
Ignacio Mendaro Corsini, Madrid
Associates:
José Ignacio Montes Herraiz,
Vicente Gonzalez Laguillo,
Mariano Martín
Supervision:
Jesús Higueras Diez, Juan
Valverde, David Rodriguez
Structural planning:
Julio Garcia Maroto
Completion: 1999

Ignacio Mendaro Corsini
Born 1946 in Marquina;
1976–96 professor at the University
of Madrid.

mendaro@telefonica.net

Shop Entrance in New York

Client:
Comme des Garçons
Architects:
Future Systems, London
Jan Kaplicky, Amanda Levete
Structural planning:
Ove Arup & Partners, London
Completion: 1998

Jan Kaplicky
Born 1937 in Prague; 1969–79
Work under Richard Rogers,
Renzo Piano, Foster Associates and
others; 1979 foundation of Future
Systems in London.

Amanda Levete
Born 1955 in Bridgend,
Great Britain; 1982–89 work under
Richard Rogers and others;
since 1989 partner at Future
Systems.

www.future-systems.com

Yellow house in Flims

Client:
Communtity of Flims
Architect:
Valerio Olgiati, Zurich
Associates:
Iris Dätwyler, Pascal Flammer,
Karen Wassung, Raphael Zuber
Supervision:
Archobau, Chur
Peter Diggelmann, Walter Carigiet
Structural planning:
Conzett, Bronzini, Gartmann, Chur
Completion: 1999

Valerio Olgiati
Born 1958 in Chur; independent
office since 1988;
1993–96 partnership with Frank
Escher in Los Angeles; 1998–2000
guest lecturer at the ETH Zurich
and at the AA London;
since 2002 professor at the
Accademia di architettura in
Mendrisio.

www.olgiati.net

Church Community Centre in Schwindkirchen

Client:
Catholic Parish Foundation
Mariä Himmelfahrt, Schwindkirchen,
Responsible authority:
Archiepiscopal office of construc-
tion and public works,
Munich/Freising
Architects:
arc Architects, Munich/Bad
Birnbach; Horst Biesterfeld,
Manfred Brennecke, Christof Illig,
Thomas Richter
Associates:
Ursula Reiter, Anke Pfeffer
Structural planning:
Seeberger, Friedl und Partner,
Pfarrkirchen/Munich
Completion: 2001

Horst Biesterfeld
Born 1940 in Cologne; since 1973
Partner at arc.

Manfred Brennecke
Born 1943 in Vienna; since 1973
Partner at arc.

Christof Illig
Born 1961 in Gießen; since 1994
Partner at arc.

Thomas Richter
Born 1941 in Munich; since
1973 Partner at arc.

www.arcArchitekten.de

Loft Conversion in Berlin

Client:
Schmitt Stumpf Frühauf und Partner, Munich
Architects:
Rudolf + Sohn Architects, Munich
Manfred Rudolf, Christine Sohn
Structural planning:
Schmitt Stumpf Frühauf und Partner, Munich
Completion: 1997

Manfred Rudolf
Born 1958; 1986–94 associate at various architecture firms;
1994–95 assistant at the Technical University of Munich; since 1994 office partnership with Christine Sohn.

Christine Sohn
Born 1964; 1990–94 associate at various architecture firms;
since 1994 office partnership with Manfred Rudolf; since 2002 scientific associate at the Technical University of Munich.

info@rudolfsohn.de

House Extension in München

Client:
Private
Architects:
Lydia Haack + John Höpfner. Architects, Munich
Structural planning:
Timotheus Brengelmann, Munich
Completion: 1999

Lydia Haack
Born 1965 in Hof; since 1996 office partnership with John Höpfner.

John Höpfner
Born 1963 in Munich; since 1996 office partnership with Lydia Haack.

www.haackhoepfner.com

House Extension in Remscheid

Client:
Private
Architects:
Gerhard Kalhöfer, Stefan Korschildgen, Cologne
Associates:
Andreas Hack
Structural planning:
Thomas Hoffmann, Cologne
Completion: 1997

Gerhard Kalhöfer
Born 1962; teaching at various universities; since 1989 professor at the FH Mainz.

Stefan Korschildgen
Born 1962; teaching at various universities; since 2001 professor at the FH Düsseldorf.

www.kalhoefer-korschildgen.de

Restaurant in Oporto

Client:
Alves, Costa, Reis, L.D.A.
Architect:
Guilherme Páris Couto, Oporto
Structural planning:
António José Costa Leite, Oporto
Completion: 1997

Guilherme Páris Couto
Born in 1964; 1993–99 associate at the architecture office of Álvaro Siza Viera; since 1997 collaboration with Magalhães Carneiro Gabinete.

guilhermepariscouto@hotmail.com

House Extension in Montrouge

Client:
Private
Architects:
Fabienne Couvert & Guillaume Terver Architects, Paris
Design in collaboration with:
IN SITU montréal, Montreal
Associates:
Marianne Bär, Aude Moynot, Martin Otto
Structural planning:
Fabienne Couvert & Guillaume Terver Architects
Completion: 1999

Fabienne Couvert
Since 1996 collaboration with Guillaume Terver; independent office since 2000.

Guillaume Terver
Since 1996 collaboration with Fabienne Couvert; independent office since 2000.

www.couverterver-architectes.com

House on Lake Starnberg

Client:
Private
Architects:
Fink + Jocher, Munich
Dietrich Fink, Thomas Jocher
Project management:
Bettina Görgner
Supervision:
Fink + Jocher with Christof Wallner, Munich
Structural planning:
Joachim Eiermann, Munich
Completion: 2000

Dietmar Fink
Born 1958 in Burgau; 1987–88 office partnership with Karlheinz Brombeiß and Nikolaus Harder; since 1991 office partnership with Thomas Jocher; since 1999 professor at TU Berlin.

Thomas Jocher
Born 1952 in Benediktbeuern; since 1991 office partnership with Dietrich Fink; since 1997 professor at Stuttgart University.

www.fink-jocher.de

Parasite in Rotterdam

Client:
Parasite Foundation in Collaboration with the Foundation Rotterdam 2001
Architects:
Korteknie Stuhlmacher Architects, Rotterdam
Rien Korteknie, Mechthild Stuhlmacher
Associates:
Iris Pennock, Marijn Mees
Structural planning:
Ingenieurbüro ARIN, Breda
Ingenieurbüro Maderholz, Donaueschingen
Merk Holzbau, Aichach
Completion: 2001

Rien Korteknie
Born 1961 in Kortgene, The Netherlands; since 1997 freelance collaboration with Mechthild Stuhlmacher; since 1997 guest lecturer at the TU Delft; independent office, Korteknie Stuhlmacher Architects, since 2001.

Mechthild Stuhlmacher
Born 1963 in Tübingen; since 1997 freelance architect, publicist and curator; since 1997 guest lecturer at TU Delft; independent office, Kortenknie Stuhlmacher Architects, since 2001.

www.ksar.nl
www.parasites.nl

Panel Construction Housing in Dresden

Client:
Wohnbau NordWest GmbH, Dresden
Architects:
Architekturbüro Knerer & Lang, Dresden
Thomas Knerer, Eva Maria Lang
Associates:
Sandra Kavelly, Frank Käpplinger, Christiane Butt
Structural planning:
Ingenieurbüro Jenewein, Dresden
Ingenieurbüro Dietrich, Dresden
Completion: 1996–2001

Thomas Knerer
Born 1963 in Garmisch-Partenkirchen; 1993 foundation of office with Eva Maria Lang; since 1999 professor at the Westsächsische Hochschule in Zwickau (FH).

Eva Maria Lang
Born 1964 in Munich; 1993 foundation of office with Thomas Knerer; since 1994 various teaching assignments, a.o. guest lecturer at the TU Dresden.

www.knererlang.de

House Development in Chur

Client:
Helvetia-Patria insurance company,
St.Gallen
Architects:
Dieter Jüngling and Andreas
Hagmann, Chur
Structural planning:
Georg Liesch AG, Chur
Completion: 2000

Dieter Jüngling
Born 1957 in Basle; associate at
Herzog & de Meuron and Peter
Zumthor; since 1990 office
partnership with Andreas Hagmann.

Andreas Hagmann
Born 1959 in Lucerne; associate at
architecture office of Peter Zumthor;
since 1990 office partnership with
Dieter Jüngling; since 1999 lecturer
at the Hochschule für Wirtschaft
und Technik in Chur.

juengling.hagmann@bluewin.ch

Museum Alf Lechner
in Ingolstadt

Client:
The City of Ingolstadt,
Foundation Museum Alf Lechner
Architects:
Fischer Architects, Munich
Florian Fischer
Associates:
Ralf Emmerling, Sieglinde Neyer
Structural planning:
Muck Ingenieure, Ingolstadt
Completion: 2000

Florian Fischer
Born 1965 in Munich; 1997
office partnership with Erhard
Fischer; since 2003 guest lecturer
at the University of Hanover;
since 2003 Florian Fischer
Architects.

www.fischer-architekten.com

Tate Modern in London

Client:
Tate Gallery
Architects:
Herzog & de Meuron, Basle
Jacques Herzog, Pierre de Meuron
Harry Gugger, Christine Binswanger
Project manager:
Michael Casey
Supervision:
Sheppard Robson + Partners,
London
Structural planning:
Ove Arup and Partners, London
Interior design:
Herzog & de Meuron
with Office for design, London
Landscape planning:
Herzog & de Meuron
with Kienast Vogt + Partner, Zurich
Completion: 1999

Jacques Herzog
Born 1950 in Basle, Switzerland;
since 1978 office partnership with
Pierre de Meuron; since 1999
professor at the ETH-Studios, Basle.

Pierre de Meuron
Born 1950 in Basle, Switzerland;
since 1978 office partnership with
Jacques Herzog; since 1999
professor at the ETH-Studios, Basle.

info@herzogdemeuron.ch

Documentation Centre in
Nuremberg

Client:
The City of Nuremberg,
Hochbauamt
Architect:
Günther Domenig, Graz
Associates:
Gerhard Wallner, Sandra Harrich
Project manager:
Hochbauamt Nürnberg
Supervision:
Rudolf Bromberger, Nuremberg
Structural planning:
Rieger + Brandt, Nuremberg
Completion: 2001

Günther Domenig
Born 1934 in Klagenfurt;
1963–73 office partnership with
Eilfried Huth; since 1973 studios in
Graz, Klagenfurt and
Vienna; since 1998 office partner-
ship with Hermann Eisenköck and
Herfried Peyker Architektur
Consult ZT GmbH.

www.archconsult.com

Insurance Building in Munich

Client:
Münchener Rückversicherungs-
Gesellschaft
Architects:
Baumschlager & Eberle, Vaduz
Carlo Baumschlager, Dietmar Eberle
Project manager:
Eckehart Loidolt, Christian
Tabernigg
Associates:
Marlies Sofia, Elmar Hasler, Alexia
Monauni, Marc Fisler, Bernhard
Demmel, Daniela Weber
Supervision:
BIP Beratende Ingenieure, Munich
Structural planning:
FSIT Friedrich Straß, Munich
Facade planning:
Wörner + Partner, Darmstadt
Landscape planning:
KVP Vogt Landscape architects,
Zurich
Completion: 2002

Carlo Baumschlager
Born 1956; since 1985
office partnership with Dietmar
Eberle; teaching since 1985.

Dietmar Eberle
Born 1952; since 1985
office partnership with Carlo
Baumschlager; teaching since
1983; since 1999 professor at the
ETH Zurich.

office@be-g.com

MoMA QNS in New York

Client:
Museum of Modern Art, New York
Architects:
Michael Maltzan Architecture, Los
Angeles (lobby, roofscape, facade)
Michael Maltzan
Project designer: Kurt Sattler
Project manager:
Brian Cavanaugh
Associates:
Dana Bauer, Nora Gordon,
Michael Schulman
in collaboration with:
Cooper, Robertson & Partners,
New York (library, depot, facade)
Project partner: Scott Newman
Project manager: Adele Finer
Associates: K. Dietz, A. Truong-
Montgomery, H. Hayakawa,
E. Boorstyn, H. Azar, W. Lin
Structural planning:
De Nardis Associates, New York
Lighting designed:
George Sexton Associates,
Washington D.C.
Completion: 2002

Michael Maltzan
Born 1959 in Long Island, USA;
independent office since 1995;
teaching at the Rhode Island School
of Design, University of Southern
California and Harvard University.

www.mmaltzan.com

Cultural and Business Centre
in Turin

Clients:
Lingotto S.p.A. and Palazzo Grassi
Architects:
Renzo Piano Building Workshop,
Genoa
Renzo Piano
Project manager: M. van der Staay
Associates:
A. Belvedere, K. van Casteren,
D. Dorell, F. Florena,
B. Plattner, A. Alborghetti,
M. Parravicini, A. H. Temenides,
C. Colson, Y. Kyrkos, O. Aubert
Structural planning:
Fiat engineering
(principal structure),
RFR (roof structure)
Completion: 2002

Renzo Piano
Born 1937 in Genoa; 1971–77
office partnership with Richard
Rogers, 1977–93 office partnership
with Peter Rice; since 1993 Renzo
Piano Building Workshop with
offices in Genoa and Paris.

www.rpbw.com

British Museum Courtyard
in London

Client:
British Museum
Architects:
Foster and Partners, London
Norman Foster, Spencer de Grey,
Giles Robinson
Structural planning:
Büro Happold, London
Mike Cook
Acoustics engineer:
Sandy Brown Associates, London
Lighting:
Claude Engle Lighting Consultant,
Maryland
Facade consultants:
Emmer Pfenniger,
CH-Munchenstein
Completion: 2000

Norman Foster
Born 1935 in Manchester; 1961
Foundation of Team 4 with Richard
Rogers; since 1967 Foster
Associates.

www.fosterandpartners.com

Authors

Christian Schittich

Born 1956
Studied architecture at the Technical University, Munich, followed by seven years of practical experience in the field; publicist; since 1991 member of the editorial team of DETAIL, since 1992, co-editor; since 1998 editor in chief; author and editor of numerous books and journal articles.

Berthold Burkhardt

Born 1941
Studied architecture and engineering in Stuttgart and Berlin;
since 1966 associate at Frei Otto;
since 1984 professor at the Institute for Structural Planning
at the TU Braunschweig;
research and teaching topics: Structural planning, light construction,
history of construction, construction and heritage protection;
architecture and engineering firm in partnership with
Martin Schumacher in Braunschweig;
publications on renovating buildings from the modern era,
history of light construction.

Johann Jessen

Born 1949
Studied architecture and urban planning at the TH Darmstadt;
professor for foundations of local and regional planning at the Institute for
Urban Planning at Stuttgart University;
active in: research in urbanism and urban planning, planning consultation;
numerous publications on urban development, urban design and planning.

Günter Moewes

Born 1935
Professor (emeritus) of Architectural Design
and Construction at Fachhochschule Dortmund;
areas of special interest: ecological building, interaction
between economy and architecture; numerous publications.

Jochem Schneider

Born 1964
Architect and urban planner;
1994–1999 associate at the Institute for Foundations
in Modern Architecture and Design at Stuttgart University;
research areas: public space, conversion and urban development;
since 1999 "raumbureau" urban planning office in Stuttgart,
projects in the area of urban planning, research and communication.

Illustration credits

The authors and editor wish to extend their sincere thanks to all those who helped to realize this book by making illustrations available. All drawings contained in this volume have been specially prepared in–house. Photos without credits are form the architects' own archives or the archives of "DETAIL, Review of Architecture". Despite intense efforts, it was not possible to identify the copyright owners of certain photos and illustrations. Their rights remain unaffected, however, and we request them to contact us.

from photographers, photo archives and image agencies:
- Archiv Autounion, Ingolstadt: p. 124
- Archiv Lingotto, Turin: pp. 144–146
- Bauhaus-Archiv Berlin; Theiss, Dessau: p. 31
- Bonfig, Peter, München: pp. 73–75
- Borges de Araujo, Nuno, Braga: pp. 102–105
- Bousema, Anne, Rotterdam: pp. 98–101
- Bruchhaus/Lachenmann, München: pp. 115, 118
- Cano, Enrico, Como: pp. 148–149, 152–153, 155
- Casals, Lluís, Barcelona: pp. 42–49
- Christillin, Cristiano, Turin: pp. 150–151
- Collovà, Roberto, Palermo: pp. 38–41
- Davies, Richard, London: pp. 55, 57
- Deutsche Foamglas GmbH, Vogt; Dirk, Haan: p. 32
- Engels, Hans, München: p. 28
- Feiner, Ralph, Malans: pp. 112
- Fessy, George, Paris: pp. 14
- Heinrich, Michael, München: pp. 89–93, 125–129
- Hinrichs, Johann, München: pp. 84–87
- Hofmann, Patrick, Bülach: p. 27
- Hueber, Eduard, New York: pp. 117, 121, 122–123
- Huthmacher, Werner/artur, Köln: pp. 59, 61–63
- Kaltenbach, Frank, München: pp. 10, 25, 119–120
- Kerez, Christian; Olgiati, Valerio, Zürich: pp. 64–67
- Landecy, Jean-Michel, Genf: p. 140
- Lange, Jörg, Wuppertal: pp. 94–97

- Lewis, Xavier, Paris: p. 83
- Malagamba, Duccio, Barcelona: p. 8
- Martinez, Ignacio, Lustenau: p. 24 bottom
- Müller, Stefan, Berlin: pp. 76–78
- Naas & Bisig, Basel: pp. 68–71
- Pradel, David, Paris: p. 20
- Prokschi, Werner, München: p. 26
- Reisch, Michael, Düsseldorf: p. 19 bottom left
- Reuss, Wolfgang, Berlin: p. 30
- Richters, Christian, Münster: pp. 130–135, 141 top right
- Roth, Lukas, Köln: p. 22
- Ruemenapf, Jan, Karlsruhe: p. 19 top left
- Schenk & Campell, Lüen: p. 111
- Schittich, Christian, München: pp. 36, 54, 139, 143 bottom right, 147
- Shinkenshiku–sha, Tokio: pp. 138 middle left, 141 bottom right, 142
- Spiluttini, Margherita, Wien: p. 138 bottom left
- Stadtbild; Petras, Christoph, Angermünde: p. 18
- Stadt Dessau, Untere Denkmal-schutzbehörde; Peter Kühn, Dessau: p. 35
- Städtische Galerie im Lenbach-haus, München: p.17
- Stahl, Heiko; Museen der Stadt Nürnberg: p. 156
- Steiner, Petra, Berlin: pp. 106–109
- Suzuki, Hisao, Barcelona: p. 51–53
- Tate Photography; Leith, Markus, London 2002: pp. 136–137
- Trapp, Tobias, Oldenburg: p. 16
- van Viegen, Maarten, Maastricht: p. 13
- von Sternberg, Morley, London: pp. 168–169
- Wessely, Heide, München: p. 167
- Wicky, Gaston, Zürich: p. 21
- Wirtgen, Steffen, Radebeul: p. 24 top
- Young, Nigel, London: pp. 165–166, 171
- Zugmann, Gerald, Wien: pp. 156–161, 163

from books and journals:
- Bauwelt 31/32, 1997, p.1761: p. 12, 2.3
- Byggekunst 2, 2002, p. 35: p. 12, 2.2

Articles and introductory b/w photos:
- p. 8; Hotel in former monastery Santa Maria do Bouro, Braga, Portugal; Eduardo Souto de Moura with Humberto Vieira, Porto
- p. 10; Headquarters of Mün-chener Rück, Munich; Baum-schlager + Eberle, Vaduz
- p. 22; Apartment and commerce building in Cologne; Brandlhuber & Kniess, Cologne
- p. 28; Bauhaus building in Dessau, Walter Gropius
- p. 36; Culture and Business centre in former Fiat factory Lingotto, Turin; Renzo Piano Building Workshop, Genua

Dust-jacket photo:
British Museum Courtyard in London
Architects:
Foster and Partners, London
Photo: Christian Schittich